MznLnx

Missing Links Exam Preps

Exam Prep for

Management: Skills and Application

Rue & Byars, 13th Edition

The MznLnx Exam Prep is your link from the texbook and lecture to your exams.
The MznLnx Exam Preps are unauthorized and comprehensive reviews of your textbooks.

All material provided by MznLnx and Rico Publications (c) 2010
Textbook publishers and textbook authors do not particpate in or contribute to these reviews.

MznLnx

Rico
Publications

Exam Prep for Management: Skills and Application
13th Edition
Rue & Byars

Publisher: Raymond Houge
Assistant Editor: Michael Rouger
Text and Cover Designer: Lisa Buckner
Marketing Manager: Sara Swagger
Project Manager, Editorial Production: Jerry Emerson
Art Director: Vernon Lowerui

Product Manager: Dave Mason
Editorial Asitant: Rachel Guzmanji
Pedagogy: Debra Long
Cover Image: Jim Reed/Getty Images
Text and Cover Printer: City Printing, Inc.
Compositor: Media Mix, Inc.

(c) 2010 Rico Publications

ALL RIGHTS RESERVED. No part of this work covered by the copyright may be reproduced or used in any form or by an means--graphic, electronic, or mechanical, including photocopying, recording, taping, Web distribution, information storage, and retrieval systems, or in any other manner--without the written permission of the publisher.

Printed in the United States
ISBN:

For more information about our products, contact us at:
Dave.Mason@RicoPublications.com

For permission to use material from this text or product, submit a request online to:
Dave.Mason@RicoPublications.com

Contents

CHAPTER 1
Management in a Diverse Workplace ... 1

CHAPTER 2
The Management Movement ... 6

CHAPTER 3
Developing Communication Skills ... 12

CHAPTER 4
Decision-Making Skills ... 14

CHAPTER 5
Ethical, Social, and Legal Responsibilities of Management ... 17

CHAPTER 6
International Business ... 26

CHAPTER 7
The Basics of Planning and Strategic Management ... 30

CHAPTER 8
Organizing Work ... 34

CHAPTER 9
Organizational Structure ... 38

CHAPTER 10
Understanding Work Groups and Teams ... 41

CHAPTER 11
Staffing ... 43

CHAPTER 12
Employee Training and Development ... 53

CHAPTER 13
Motivating Employees ... 56

CHAPTER 14
Developing Leadership Skills ... 60

CHAPTER 15
Managing Conflict and Stress ... 64

CHAPTER 16
Managing Change and Culture ... 67

CHAPTER 17
Management Control ... 71

CHAPTER 18
Appraising and Rewarding Performance ... 76

CHAPTER 19
Operations Management and Planning ... 80

CHAPTER 20
Operations Control ... 87

ANSWER KEY ... 96

TO THE STUDENT

COMPREHENSIVE

The *MznLnx* Exam Prep series is designed to help you pass your exams. Editors at MznLnx review your textbooks and then prepare these practice exams to help you master the textbook material. Unlike study guides, workbooks, and practice tests provided by the texbook publisher and textbook authors, *MznLnx* gives you **all** of the material in each chapter in exam form, not just samples, so you can be sure to nail your exam.

MECHANICAL

The MznLnx Exam Prep series creates exams that will help you learn the subject matter as well as test you on your understanding. Each question is designed to help you master the concept. Just working through the exams, you gain an understanding of the subject--its a simple mechanical process that produces success.

INTEGRATED STUDY GUIDE AND REVIEW

MznLnx is not just a set of exams designed to test you, its also a comprehensive review of the subject content. Each exam question is also a review of the concept, making sure that you will get the answer correct without having to go to other sources of material. You learn as you go! Its the easiest way to pass an exam.

HUMOR

Studying can be tedious and dry. MznLnx's instructional design includes moderate humor within the exam questions on occassion, to break the tedium and revitalize the brain

Chapter 1. Management in a Diverse Workplace

1. _____ has been described as the 'process of social influence in which one person can enlist the aid and support of others in the accomplishment of a common task' . A definition more inclusive of followers comes from Alan Keith of Genentech who said '_____ is ultimately about creating a way for people to contribute to making something extraordinary happen.'

   _____ is one of the most salient aspects of the organizational context. However, defining _____ has been challenging.

   a. Situational leadership
   b. 28-hour day
   c. 1990 Clean Air Act
   d. Leadership

2. _____ is a layer of management in an organization whose primary job responsibility is to monitor activities of subordinates while reporting to upper management.

   In pre-computer times, _____ would collect information from junior management and reassemble it for senior management. With the advent of inexpensive PCs this function has been taken over by e-business systems.

   a. Community management
   b. Continuous monitoring
   c. Theory Y
   d. Middle management

3. _____ is generally a team of individuals at the highest level of organizational management who have the day-to-day responsibilities of managing a corporation. There are most often higher levels of responsibility, such as a board of directors and those who own the company (shareholders), but they focus on managing the _____ instead of the day-to-day activities of the business.

   They are sometimes referred to, within corporations, as top management, upper management, higher management, or simply seniors.

   a. Crisis management
   b. Functional management
   c. Management development
   d. Senior management

Chapter 1. Management in a Diverse Workplace

4. _____ is one of the managerial functions like planning, organizing, staffing and directing. It is an important function because it helps to check the errors and to take the corrective action so that deviation from standards are minimized and stated goals of the organization are achieved in desired manner. According to modern concepts, _____ is a foreseeing action whereas earlier concept of _____ was used only when errors were detected. _____ in management means setting standards, measuring actual performance and taking corrective action.

   a. Decision tree pruning
   b. Control
   c. Schedule of reinforcement
   d. Turnover

5. Organizational culture is not the same as _____. It is wider and deeper concepts, something that an organization 'is' rather than what it 'has' (according to Buchanan and Huczynski.)

   _____ is the total sum of the values, customs, traditions and meanings that make a company unique.

   a. Path-goal theory
   b. Work design
   c. Corporate culture
   d. Job analysis

6. In the field of human resource management, _____ is the field concerned with organizational activity aimed at bettering the performance of individuals and groups in organizational settings. It has been known by several names, including employee development, human resource development, and learning and development.

   Harrison observes that the name was endlessly debated by the Chartered Institute of Personnel and Development during its review of professional standards in 1999/2000.

   a. Revolving door syndrome
   b. Person specification
   c. Training and development
   d. Performance appraisal

7. _____ can be regarded as an outcome of mental processes (cognitive process) leading to the selection of a course of action among several alternatives. Every _____ process produces a final choice. The output can be an action or an opinion of choice.

a. Decision making
b. 28-hour day
c. 1990 Clean Air Act
d. 33 Strategies of War

8. _____ Movement refers to those researchers of organizational development who study the behavior of people in groups, in particular workplace groups. It originated in the 1920s' Hawthorne studies, which examined the effects of social relations, motivation and employee satisfaction on factory productivity. The movement viewed workers in terms of their psychology and fit with companies, rather than as interchangeable parts.
   a. Hersey-Blanchard situational theory
   b. Work design
   c. Participatory management
   d. Human relations

9. _____ or _____ data refers to selected population characteristics as used in government, marketing or opinion research, or the _____ profiles used in such research. Note the distinction from the term 'demography' Commonly-used _____s include race, age, income, disabilities, mobility (in terms of travel time to work or number of vehicles available), educational attainment, home ownership, employment status, and even location.
   a. Adam Smith
   b. Demographic
   c. Affiliation
   d. Abraham Harold Maslow

10. The 'business case for _____', theorizes that in a global marketplace, a company that employs a diverse workforce (both men and women, people of many generations, people from ethnically and racially diverse backgrounds etc.) is better able to understand the demographics of the marketplace it serves and is thus better equipped to thrive in that marketplace than a company that has a more limited range of employee demographics.

An additional corollary suggests that a company that supports the _____ of its workforce can also improve employee satisfaction, productivity and retention.

   a. Kanban
   b. Diversity
   c. Virtual team
   d. Trademark

11. In economics, the term _____ refers to situations where the advancement of a qualified person within the hierarchy of an organization is stopped at a lower level because of some form of discrimination, most commonly sexism or racism, but since the term was coined, '_____' has also come to describe the limited advancement of the deaf, blind, disabled, aged and sexual minorities. It is an unofficial, invisible barrier that prevents women and minorities from advancing in businesses.

This situation is referred to as a 'ceiling' as there is a limitation blocking upward advancement, and 'glass' (transparent) because the limitation is not immediately apparent and is normally an unwritten and unofficial policy. This invisible barrier continues to exist, even though there are no explicit obstacles keeping minorities from acquiring advanced job positions - there are no advertisements that specifically say 'no minorities hired at this establishment', nor are there any formal orders that say 'minorities are not qualified' - but they do lie beneath the surface.

a. 33 Strategies of War
b. 28-hour day
c. Glass ceiling
d. 1990 Clean Air Act

12. An _____ is a person who has possession of an enterprise and assumes significant accountability for the inherent risks and the outcome. It is an ambitious leader who combines land, labor, and capital to create and market new goods or services. The term is a loanword from French and was first defined by the Irish economist Richard Cantillon.

a. A4e
b. AAAI
c. A Stake in the Outcome
d. Entrepreneur

13. _____ according to Onuoha (2007) is the practice of starting new organizations or revitalizing mature organizations, particularly new businesses generally in response to identified opportunities. _____ is often a difficult undertaking, as a vast majority of new businesses fail. Entrepreneurial activities are substantially different depending on the type of organization that is being started.

a. A Stake in the Outcome
b. AAAI
c. A4e
d. Entrepreneurship

14. _____ is the practice of using entrepreneurial skills without taking on the risks or accountability associated with entrepreneurial activities. It is practiced by employees within an established organization using a business model. Employees, perhaps engaged in a special project within a larger firm are supposed to behave as entrepreneurs, even though they have the resources and capabilities of the larger firm to draw upon.

Chapter 1. Management in a Diverse Workplace

a. Intrapreneurship
b. A4e
c. A Stake in the Outcome
d. AAAI

15. A _____ is a business that is privately owned and operated, with a small number of employees and relatively low volume of sales. The legal definition of 'small' often varies by country and industry, but is generally under 100 employees in the United States and under 50 employees in the European Union. In comparison, the definition of mid-sized business by the number of employees is generally under 500 in the U.S. and 250 for the European Union.

a. Critical Success Factor
b. Golden Boot Compensation
c. Pre-determined overhead rate
d. Small business

16. _____ is the harmful physical and emotional response that occurs when there is a poor match between job demands and the capabilities, resources, or needs of the worker.

Stress-related disorders encompass a broad array of conditions, including psychological disorders (e.g., depression, anxiety, post-traumatic stress disorder) and other types of emotional strain (e.g., dissatisfaction, fatigue, tension, etc.), maladaptive behaviors (e.g., aggression, substance abuse), and cognitive impairment (e.g., concentration and memory problems.) In turn, these conditions may lead to poor work performance or even injury.

a. 28-hour day
b. 1990 Clean Air Act
c. 33 Strategies of War
d. Workplace stress

17. The general definition of an _____ is an evaluation of a person, organization, system, process, project or product. _____s are performed to ascertain the validity and reliability of information; also to provide an assessment of a system's internal control. The goal of an _____ is to express an opinion on the person / organization/system (etc) in question, under evaluation based on work done on a test basis.

a. Internal control
b. Audit committee
c. A Stake in the Outcome
d. Audit

Chapter 2. The Management Movement

1. The _____ was a period in the late 18th and early 19th centuries when major changes in agriculture, manufacturing, mining, and transportation had a profound effect on the socioeconomic and cultural conditions in Britain. The changes subsequently spread throughout Europe, North America, and eventually the world. The onset of the _____ marked a major turning point in human society; almost every aspect of daily life was eventually influenced in some way.
   a. Affiliation
   b. Industrial Revolution
   c. Abraham Harold Maslow
   d. Adam Smith

2. A _____ or labor union is an organization of workers who have banded together to achieve common goals in key areas and working conditions. The _____, through its leadership, bargains with the employer on behalf of union members (rank and file members) and negotiates labor contracts (Collective bargaining) with employers. This may include the negotiation of wages, work rules, complaint procedures, rules governing hiring, firing and promotion of workers, benefits, workplace safety and policies.
   a. Labour law
   b. Company union
   c. Working time
   d. Trade union

3. Various _____ can be employed dependent on the culture of the business, the nature of the task, the nature of the workforce and the personality and skills of the leaders. This idea was further developed by Robert Tannenbaum and Warren H. Schmidt (1958, 1973) who argued that the style of leadership is dependent upon the prevailing circumstance; therefore leaders should exercise a range of leadership styles and should deploy them as appropriate.

   An Autocratic or authoritarian manager makes all the decisions, keeping the information and decision making among the senior management.

   a. 33 Strategies of War
   b. 1990 Clean Air Act
   c. 28-hour day
   d. Management styles

4. _____ is best described as the process from which managers learn and improve their skills not only to benefit themselves but also their employing organizations.

   In organisational development (OD), the effectiveness of management is recognised as one of the determinants of organisational success. Therefore, investment in _____ can have a direct economic benefit to the organization.

Chapter 2. The Management Movement 7

   a. Job enrichment
   b. Senior management
   c. Management development
   d. Fix it twice

5. _____ is a theory of management that analyzes and synthesizes workflows, with the objective of improving labour productivity. The core ideas of the theory were developed by Frederick Winslow Taylor in the 1880s and 1890s, and were first published in his monographs, Shop Management and The Principles of _____ Taylor believed that decisions based upon tradition and rules of thumb should be replaced by precise procedures developed after careful study of an individual at work.
   a. Master production schedule
   b. Capacity planning
   c. Value engineering
   d. Scientific management

6. The _____ requires the Federal government to investigate and pursue trusts, companies and organizations suspected of violating the Act. It was the first United States Federal statute to limit cartels and monopolies, and today still forms the basis for most antitrust litigation by the federal government.
   a. 1990 Clean Air Act
   b. Sherman Antitrust Act
   c. 33 Strategies of War
   d. 28-hour day

7. A _____ is a type of bar chart that illustrates a project schedule. _____s illustrate the start and finish dates of the terminal elements and summary elements of a project. Terminal elements and summary elements comprise the work breakdown structure of the project.
   a. 28-hour day
   b. 1990 Clean Air Act
   c. 33 Strategies of War
   d. Gantt chart

8. The _____ is a monograph published by Frederick Winslow Taylor in 1911. This influential monograph is the basis of modern organization and decision theory and has motivated administrators and students of managerial technique. Taylor was an American mechanical engineer and a management consultant in his later years.

Chapter 2. The Management Movement

   a. 33 Strategies of War
   b. Principles of Scientific Management
   c. 1990 Clean Air Act
   d. 28-hour day

9. A _____ is a list of the general tasks and responsibilities of a position. Typically, it also includes to whom the position reports, specifications such as the qualifications needed by the person in the job, salary range for the position, etc. A _____ is usually developed by conducting a job analysis, which includes examining the tasks and sequences of tasks necessary to perform the job.
   a. Job description
   b. Recruitment advertising
   c. Recruitment
   d. Recruitment Process Insourcing

10. _____ Movement refers to those researchers of organizational development who study the behavior of people in groups, in particular workplace groups. It originated in the 1920s' Hawthorne studies, which examined the effects of social relations, motivation and employee satisfaction on factory productivity. The movement viewed workers in terms of their psychology and fit with companies, rather than as interchangeable parts.
   a. Work design
   b. Human relations
   c. Participatory management
   d. Hersey-Blanchard situational theory

11. The _____ is a form of reactivity whereby subjects improve an aspect of their behavior being experimentally measured simply in response to the fact that they are being studied, not in response to any particular experimental manipulation.

The term was coined in 1955 by Henry A. Landsberger when analyzing older experiments from 1924-1932 at the Hawthorne Works (outside Chicago.) Hawthorne Works had commissioned a study to see if its workers would become more productive in higher or lower levels of light.

   a. Hawthorne effect
   b. 1990 Clean Air Act
   c. 33 Strategies of War
   d. 28-hour day

Chapter 2. The Management Movement

12. A _____ is a body of elected or appointed members who jointly oversee the activities of a company or organization. The body sometimes has a different name, such as board of trustees, board of governors, board of managers, or executive board. It is often simply referred to as 'the board.'

A board's activities are determined by the powers, duties, and responsibilities delegated to it or conferred on it by an authority outside itself.

   a. Clean Water Act
   b. Foreign Corrupt Practices Act
   c. Competition law
   d. Board of directors

13. _____ in mathematics and statistics is concerned with identifying the values, uncertainties and other issues relevant in a given decision and the resulting optimal decision. It is sometimes called game theory.

Most of _____ is normative or prescriptive, i.e., it is concerned with identifying the best decision to take, assuming an ideal decision maker who is fully informed, able to compute with perfect accuracy, and fully rational.

   a. Nominal group technique
   b. Rational planning model
   c. Belief decision matrix
   d. Decision theory

14. _____ is a process of planning and controlling the performance or execution of any type of activity, such as:

   - a project (project _____) or
   - a process (process _____, sometimes referred to as the process performance measurement and management system.)

Organization's senior management is responsible for carrying out its _____.

   a. Work design
   b. Management process
   c. Participatory management
   d. Human Relations Movement

Chapter 2. The Management Movement

15. _____ is the name applied to two competing management theories. One was developed by Abraham H. Maslow in his book Maslow on Management and the other is Dr. William Ouchi's so-called 'Japanese Management' style popularized during the Asian economic boom of the 1980s. In contrast Theory X, which stated that workers inherently dislike and avoid work and must be driven to it, and Theory Y, which stated that work is natural and can be a source of satisfaction when aimed at higher order human psychological needs, _____ focused on increasing employee loyalty to the company by providing a job for life with a strong focus on the well-being of the employee, both on and off the job.
    a. Theory Z
    b. 1990 Clean Air Act
    c. Sustainable competitive advantage
    d. 28-hour day

16. The _____ is given by the United States National Institute of Standards and Technology. Through the actions of the National Productivity Advisory Committee chaired by Jack Grayson, it was established by the Malcolm Baldrige National Quality Improvement Act of 1987 - Public Law 100-107 and named for Malcolm Baldrige, who served as United States Secretary of Commerce during the Reagan administration from 1981 until his 1987 death in a rodeo accident. APQC, , organized the first White House Conference on Productivity, spearheading the creation and design of the _____ in 1987, and jointly administering the award for its first three years.
    a. Time and attendance
    b. Scenario planning
    c. Business Network Transformation
    d. Malcolm Baldrige National Quality Award

17. _____ is a business management strategy aimed at embedding awareness of quality in all organizational processes. _____ has been widely used in manufacturing, education, hospitals, call centers, government, and service industries, as well as NASA space and science programs.

    As defined by the International Organization for Standardization (ISO):

    '_____ is a management approach for an organization, centered on quality, based on the participation of all its members and aiming at long-term success through customer satisfaction, and benefits to all members of the organization and to society.' ISO 8402:1994

    One major aim is to reduce variation from every process so that greater consistency of effort is obtained. (Royse, D., Thyer, B., Padgett D., ' Logan T., 2006)

    a. 28-hour day
    b. Quality management
    c. 1990 Clean Air Act
    d. Total quality management

18. _____ can be considered to have three main components: quality control, quality assurance and quality improvement. _____ is focused not only on product quality, but also the means to achieve it. _____ therefore uses quality assurance and control of processes as well as products to achieve more consistent quality.
   a. 28-hour day
   b. 1990 Clean Air Act
   c. Total quality management
   d. Quality management

Chapter 3. Developing Communication Skills

1. _____ describes the situation when output from (or information about the result of) an event or phenomenon in the past will influence the same event/phenomenon in the present or future. When an event is part of a chain of cause-and-effect that forms a circuit or loop, then the event is said to 'feed back' into itself.

   _____ is also a synonym for:

   - _____ signal; the information about the initial event that is the basis for subsequent modification of the event.
   - _____ loop; the causal path that leads from the initial generation of the _____ signal to the subsequent modification of the event.

   _____ is a mechanism, process or signal that is looped back to control a system within itself. Such a loop is called a _____ loop.

   a. Feedback
   b. 1990 Clean Air Act
   c. Feedback loop
   d. Positive feedback

2. A _____ or labor union is an organization of workers who have banded together to achieve common goals in key areas and working conditions. The _____, through its leadership, bargains with the employer on behalf of union members (rank and file members) and negotiates labor contracts (Collective bargaining) with employers. This may include the negotiation of wages, work rules, complaint procedures, rules governing hiring, firing and promotion of workers, benefits, workplace safety and policies.
   a. Labour law
   b. Working time
   c. Company union
   d. Trade union

3. _____ can be regarded as an outcome of mental processes (cognitive process) leading to the selection of a course of action among several alternatives. Every _____ process produces a final choice. The output can be an action or an opinion of choice.
   a. 1990 Clean Air Act
   b. 33 Strategies of War
   c. 28-hour day
   d. Decision making

4. An _____ is a private computer network that uses Internet technologies to securely share any part of an organization's information or operational systems with its employees. Sometimes the term refers only to the organization's internal website, but often it is a more extensive part of the organization's computer infrastructure and private websites are an important component and focal point of internal communication and collaboration.

An _____ is built from the same concepts and technologies used for the Internet, such as client-server computing and the Internet Protocol Suite (TCP/IP.)

 a. Intranet
 b. AAAI
 c. A Stake in the Outcome
 d. A4e

Chapter 4. Decision-Making Skills

1. _____ can be regarded as an outcome of mental processes (cognitive process) leading to the selection of a course of action among several alternatives. Every _____ process produces a final choice. The output can be an action or an opinion of choice.
    a. 33 Strategies of War
    b. 28-hour day
    c. 1990 Clean Air Act
    d. Decision making

2. _____ is a concept based on the fact that rationality of individuals is limited by the information they have, the cognitive limitations of their minds, and the finite amount of time they have to make decisions. This contrasts with the concept of rationality as optimization. Another way to look at _____ is that, because decision-makers lack the ability and resources to arrive at the optimal solution, they instead apply their rationality only after having greatly simplified the choices available.
    a. Transferable utility
    b. Complete information
    c. Mixed strategy
    d. Bounded rationality

3. In decision theory and estimation theory, the _____ of an estimator, $\hat{\theta}$, of an unknown parameter of the distribution, θ, is the expected value of the loss function

$$R(\theta, \hat{\theta}) = \mathbb{E}_\theta L(\theta, \hat{\theta}) = \int L(\theta, \hat{\theta})\, dP_\theta.$$

where dP_θ is a probability measure parametrized by θ.

- For a scalar parameter θ and a quadratic loss function,

$$L(\theta, \hat{\theta}) = (\theta - \hat{\theta})^2$$

the _____ function becomes the mean squared error of the estimate,

$$R(\theta, \hat{\theta}) = E_\theta(\theta - \hat{\theta})^2$$

- In density estimation, the unknown parameter is probability density itself. The loss function is typically chosen to be a norm in an appropriate function space. For example, for L^2 norm,

$$L(f, \hat{f}) = \|f - \hat{f}\|_2^2$$

the _____ function becomes the mean integrated squared error

$$R(f, \hat{f}) = E\|f - \hat{f}\|^2$$

a. Linear model
b. Risk aversion
c. Financial modeling
d. Risk

4. _____ is a group creativity technique designed to generate a large number of ideas for the solution of a problem. The method was first popularized in the late 1930s by Alex Faickney Osborn in a book called Applied Imagination. Osborn proposed that groups could double their creative output with _____.
a. Abraham Harold Maslow
b. Adam Smith
c. Brainstorming
d. Affiliation

5. The _____ is a decision making method for use among groups of many sizes, who want to make their decision quickly, as by a vote, but want everyone's opinions taken into account (as opposed to traditional voting, where only the largest group is considered). The method of tallying is the difference. First, every member of the group gives their view of the solution, with a short explanation.

a. Belief decision matrix
b. Hierarchical Decision Process
c. Decision model
d. Nominal group technique

6. 6-3-5 _____ is a group creativity technique used in marketing, advertising, design, writing and product development originally developed by Professor Bernd Rohrbach in 1968.

Based on the concept of Brainstorming, the aim of 6-3-5 _____ is to generate 108 new ideas in half an hour. In a similar way to brainstorming, it is not the quality of ideas that matters but the quantity.

The technique involves 6 participants who sit in a group and are supervised by a moderator. Each participant thinks up 3 ideas every 5 minutes. Participants are encouraged to draw on others' ideas for inspiration, thus stimulating the creative process. After 6 rounds in 30 minutes the group has thought up a total of 108 ideas.

a. Brainwriting
b. 33 Strategies of War
c. 1990 Clean Air Act
d. 28-hour day

7. A _____ is a subset of the overall internal controls of a business covering the application of people, documents, technologies, and procedures by management accountants to solving business problems such as costing a product, service or a business-wide strategy. _____s are distinct from regular information systems in that they are used to analyze other information systems applied in operational activities in the organization. Academically, the term is commonly used to refer to the group of information management methods tied to the automation or support of human decision making, e.g. Decision Support Systems, Expert systems, and Executive information systems.

a. Strategic information system
b. 28-hour day
c. 1990 Clean Air Act
d. Management information system

Chapter 5. Ethical, Social, and Legal Responsibilities of Management

1. The _____ is an American federal law which allows people who are not affiliated with the government to file actions against federal contractors claiming fraud against the government. The act of filing such actions is informally called 'whistleblowing.' Persons filing under the Act stand to receive a portion (usually about 15-25 percent) of any recovered damages.
    a. Bennett Amendment
    b. Chrapliwy v. Uniroyal
    c. False Claims Act
    d. Personal Responsibility and Work Opportunity Reconciliation Act

2. An _____ is any party that makes an investment.

    The term has taken on a specific meaning in finance to describe the particular types of people and companies that regularly purchase equity or debt securities for financial gain in exchange for funding an expanding company. Less frequently, the term is applied to parties who purchase real estate, currency, commodity derivatives, personal property, or other assets.

    a. A Stake in the Outcome
    b. A4e
    c. AAAI
    d. Investor

3. _____ is the harmful physical and emotional response that occurs when there is a poor match between job demands and the capabilities, resources, or needs of the worker.

    Stress-related disorders encompass a broad array of conditions, including psychological disorders (e.g., depression, anxiety, post-traumatic stress disorder) and other types of emotional strain (e.g., dissatisfaction, fatigue, tension, etc.), maladaptive behaviors (e.g., aggression, substance abuse), and cognitive impairment (e.g:, concentration and memory problems.) In turn, these conditions may lead to poor work performance or even injury.

    a. 33 Strategies of War
    b. 28-hour day
    c. 1990 Clean Air Act
    d. Workplace stress

4. Organizational culture is not the same as _____. It is wider and deeper concepts, something that an organization 'is' rather than what it 'has' (according to Buchanan and Huczynski.)

    _____ is the total sum of the values, customs, traditions and meanings that make a company unique.

Chapter 5. Ethical, Social, and Legal Responsibilities of Management

   a. Corporate culture
   b. Work design
   c. Path-goal theory
   d. Job analysis

5. In the field of human resource management, _____ is the field concerned with organizational activity aimed at bettering the performance of individuals and groups in organizational settings. It has been known by several names, including employee development, human resource development, and learning and development.

Harrison observes that the name was endlessly debated by the Chartered Institute of Personnel and Development during its review of professional standards in 1999/2000.

   a. Revolving door syndrome
   b. Performance appraisal
   c. Person specification
   d. Training and development

6. _____ is a broad label that refers to any individuals or households that use goods and services generated within the economy. The concept of a _____ is used in different contexts, so that the usage and significance of the term may vary.

Typically when business people and economists talk of _____s they are talking about person as _____, an aggregated commodity item with little individuality other than that expressed in the buy/not-buy decision.

   a. 33 Strategies of War
   b. 28-hour day
   c. 1990 Clean Air Act
   d. Consumer

7. _____ laws are designed to ensure fair competition and the free flow of truthful information in the marketplace. The laws are designed to prevent businesses that engage in fraud or specified unfair practices from gaining an advantage over competitors and may provide additional protection for the weak and unable to take care of themselves. _____ laws are a form of government regulation which protects the interests of consumers.
   a. Certificate of Incorporation
   b. Consumer protection
   c. Comprehensive Environmental Response, Compensation, and Liability Act
   d. Sarbanes-Oxley Act

Chapter 5. Ethical, Social, and Legal Responsibilities of Management

8. The _____ is an independent agency of the United States government, established in 1914 by the _____ Act. Its principal mission is the promotion of 'consumer protection' and the elimination and prevention of what regulators perceive to be harmfully 'anti-competitive' business practices, such as coercive monopoly.

The _____ Act was one of President Wilson's major acts against trusts.

   a. 28-hour day
   b. 1990 Clean Air Act
   c. Federal Trade Commission
   d. 33 Strategies of War

9. The _____ requires the Federal government to investigate and pursue trusts, companies and organizations suspected of violating the Act. It was the first United States Federal statute to limit cartels and monopolies, and today still forms the basis for most antitrust litigation by the federal government.
   a. 1990 Clean Air Act
   b. 28-hour day
   c. 33 Strategies of War
   d. Sherman Antitrust Act

10. The _____ of 1938 is a United States federal law that amended the Federal Trade Commission Act to add the clause 'unfair or deceptive acts or practices in commerce are hereby declared unlawful' to the Section 5 prohibition of unfair methods of competition, in order to protect consumers as well as competition.

1938 amendment to the federal trade commission act that authorized the FTC to restrict unfair or deceptive acts; also called the advertising act. Until this amendment was passed, the FTC could only restrict practices that were unfair to competitors.

   a. Drug test
   b. Reverification
   c. Financial Security Law of France
   d. Wheeler-Lea Act

11. In finance, an _____ is a contract between a buyer and a seller that gives the buyer the right--but not the obligation-- to buy or to sell a particular asset (the underlying asset) at a later day at an agreed price. In return for granting the _____, the seller collects a payment (the premium) from the buyer. A call _____ gives the buyer the right to buy the underlying asset; a put _____ gives the buyer of the _____ the right to sell the underlying asset.

Chapter 5. Ethical, Social, and Legal Responsibilities of Management

   a. A4e
   b. AAAI
   c. A Stake in the Outcome
   d. Option

12. A _____ is a relatively new executive level position at a corporation, company, organization typically reporting directly to the CEO or board of directors. The _____ is responsible for a brand's image, experience, and promise, and propagating it throughout all aspects of the company. The brand officer oversees marketing, advertising, design, public relations and customer service departments.
    a. Director of communications
    b. Chief brand officer
    c. Purchasing manager
    d. Chief executive officer

13. The _____ is the primary federal law in the United States governing water pollution. The act established the symbolic goals of eliminating releases to water of high amounts of toxic substances, eliminating additional water pollution by 1985, and ensuring that surface waters would meet standards necessary for human sports and recreation by 1983.

    The principal body of law currently in effect is based on the Federal Water Pollution Control Amendments of 1972, which significantly expanded and strengthened earlier legislation.

    a. Non-disclosure agreement
    b. Clean Water Act
    c. Foreign Corrupt Practices Act
    d. Regulatory compliance

14. The United States _____ is an independent agency of the United States government created in 1972 through the Consumer Product Safety Act to protect 'against unreasonable risks of injuries associated with consumer products.' As of 2006 its acting chairman is Nancy Nord, a Republican. The other commissioner is Thomas Hill Moore, a Democrat. Normally the board has three commissioners.
    a. 28-hour day
    b. 33 Strategies of War
    c. Consumer Product Safety Commission
    d. 1990 Clean Air Act

Chapter 5. Ethical, Social, and Legal Responsibilities of Management

15. _____ is one of the managerial functions like planning, organizing, staffing and directing. It is an important function because it helps to check the errors and to take the corrective action so that deviation from standards are minimized and stated goals of the organization are achieved in desired manner. According to modern concepts, _____ is a foreseeing action whereas earlier concept of _____ was used only when errors were detected. _____ in management means setting standards, measuring actual performance and taking corrective action.
    a. Control
    b. Turnover
    c. Decision tree pruning
    d. Schedule of reinforcement

16. The United States Federal _____ to oversee the safety of food, drugs, and cosmetics. A principal author of this law was Royal S. Copeland, a three-term U.S. Senator from New York. In 1968, the Electronic Product Radiation Control provisions were added to the FD'C.
    a. Food, Drug, and Cosmetic Act
    b. Comprehensive Environmental Response, Compensation, and Liability Act
    c. Rulemaking
    d. Partnership

17. A _____ is typically described as a deliberate plan of action to guide decisions and achieve rational outcome(s.) However, the term may also be used to denote what is actually done, even though it is unplanned.

    The term may apply to government, private sector organizations and groups, and individuals.

    a. 1990 Clean Air Act
    b. 33 Strategies of War
    c. Policy
    d. 28-hour day

18. The _____ is a United States law, passed by the United States Congress in 1976, that regulates the introduction of new or already existing chemicals. It grandfathered most existing chemicals, in contrast to the Registration, Evaluation and Authorization of Chemicals (REACH) legislation of the European Union. However, as explained below, the _____ specifically regulates polychlorinated biphenyl (PCB) products.
    a. Drug test
    b. Toxic Substances Control Act
    c. Federal Employers Liability Act
    d. National treatment

19. The _____ of 1968 is a United States federal law designed to protect consumers in credit transactions, by requiring clear disclosure of key terms of the lending arrangement and all costs. The statute is contained in Title I of the Consumer Credit Protection Act, as amended (15 U.S.C. Â§ 1601 et seq.).
   a. 1990 Clean Air Act
   b. Truth in Lending Act
   c. Fair Credit Reporting Act
   d. 28-hour day

20. _____ are legal property rights over creations of the mind, both artistic and commercial, and the corresponding fields of law. Under _____ law, owners are granted certain exclusive rights to a variety of intangible assets, such as musical, literary, and artistic works; ideas, discoveries and inventions; and words, phrases, symbols, and designs. Common types of _____ include copyrights, trademarks, patents, industrial design rights and trade secrets.
   a. Equal Pay Act
   b. Intellectual property
   c. Intent
   d. Unemployment Action Center

21. _____ plant, and equipment, is a term used in accountancy for assets and property which cannot easily be converted into cash. This can be compared with current assets such as cash or bank accounts, which are described as liquid assets. In most cases, only tangible assets are referred to as fixed.
   a. 33 Strategies of War
   b. 28-hour day
   c. 1990 Clean Air Act
   d. Fixed asset

22. The 'business case for _____', theorizes that in a global marketplace, a company that employs a diverse workforce (both men and women, people of many generations, people from ethnically and racially diverse backgrounds etc.) is better able to understand the demographics of the marketplace it serves and is thus better equipped to thrive in that marketplace than a company that has a more limited range of employee demographics.

An additional corollary suggests that a company that supports the _____ of its workforce can also improve employee satisfaction, productivity and retention.

   a. Virtual team
   b. Trademark
   c. Diversity
   d. Kanban

23. The general definition of an _____ is an evaluation of a person, organization, system, process, project or product. _____s are performed to ascertain the validity and reliability of information; also to provide an assessment of a system's internal control. The goal of an _____ is to express an opinion on the person / organization/system (etc) in question, under evaluation based on work done on a test basis.
    a. Internal control
    b. A Stake in the Outcome
    c. Audit
    d. Audit committee

24. A _____ also known as a sole trader, or simply proprietorship is a type of business entity which there is only one owner and he has the final word taking all desicions by himself. All debts of the business are debts of the owner and must pay from his personal possessions. This means that the owner has unlimited liabilty.
    a. Sole proprietorship
    b. Golden hello
    c. Business rule
    d. Foreign ownership

25. A _____ is a type of business entity in which partners (owners) share with each other the profits or losses of the business. _____s are often favored over corporations for taxation purposes, as the _____ structure does not generally incur a tax on profits before it is distributed to the partners (i.e. there is no dividend tax levied.) However, depending on the _____ structure and the jurisdiction in which it operates, owners of a _____ may be exposed to greater personal liability than they would as shareholders of a corporation.
    a. Partnership
    b. Federal Employers Liability Act
    c. Mediation
    d. Due process

26. An _____ is a tax levied on the financial income of people, corporations, or other legal entities. Various _____ systems exist, with varying degrees of tax incidence. Income taxation can be progressive, proportional, or regressive.
    a. A Stake in the Outcome
    b. Income tax
    c. A4e
    d. Ordinary income

27. A _____ is a set of exclusive rights granted by a state to an inventor or his assignee for a limited period of time in exchange for a disclosure of an invention.

24   *Chapter 5. Ethical, Social, and Legal Responsibilities of Management*

The procedure for granting _____s, the requirements placed on the _____ee and the extent of the exclusive rights vary widely between countries according to national laws and international agreements. Typically, however, a _____ application must include one or more claims defining the invention which must be new, inventive, and useful or industrially applicable.

   a. Food, Drug, and Cosmetic Act
   b. Federal Trade Commission Act
   c. Labor Management Reporting and Disclosure Act
   d. Patent

28. A _____ is a distinctive sign or indicator used by an individual, business organization, or other legal entity to identify that the products and/or services to consumers with which the _____ appears originate from a unique source and to distinguish its products or services from those of other entities.
   a. Virtual team
   b. Kanban
   c. Trademark
   d. Succession planning

29. The _____ is a US law that applies to labels on many consumer products. It requires the label to state:

- The identity of the product;
- The name and place of business of the manufacturer, packer, or distributor; and
- The net quantity of contents.

The contents statement must include both metric and U.S. customary units.

Passed under Lyndon B. Johnson in 1966, the law first took effect on July 1, 1967. The metric labeling requirement was added in 1992 and took effect on February 14, 1994.

   a. 33 Strategies of War
   b. 28-hour day
   c. 1990 Clean Air Act
   d. Fair Packaging and Labeling Act

30. _____ is the science, art and technology of enclosing or protecting products for distribution, storage, sale, and use. _____ also refers to the process of design, evaluation, and production of packages. _____ can be described as a coordinated system of preparing goods for transport, warehousing, logistics, sale, and end use.

a. Supply chain
b. Supply chain management
c. Packaging
d. Wholesalers

31. _____ is a method of direct marketing in which a salesperson solicits to prospective customers to buy products or services, either over the phone or through a subsequent face to face or Web conferencing appointment scheduled during the call.

_____ can also include recorded sales pitches programmed to be played over the phone via automatic dialing. _____ has come under fire in recent years, being viewed as an annoyance by many.

a. 33 Strategies of War
b. Telemarketing
c. 28-hour day
d. 1990 Clean Air Act

32. The _____, first published in 1952, is one of a number of uniform acts that have been promulgated in conjunction with efforts to harmonize the law of sales and other commercial transactions in all 50 states within the United States of America. This objective is deemed important because of the prevalence of commercial transactions that extend beyond one state (for example, where the goods are manufactured in state A, warehoused in state B, sold from state C and delivered in state D.) The _____ deals primarily with transactions involving personal property (movable property), not real property (immovable property.)

a. Uniform Commercial Code
b. AAAI
c. A4e
d. A Stake in the Outcome

Chapter 6. International Business

1. _____ is exchange of capital, goods, and services across international borders or territories. In most countries, it represents a significant share of gross domestic product (GDP.) While _____ has been present throughout much of history, its economic, social, and political importance has been on the rise in recent centuries.
   a. A4e
   b. AAAI
   c. International trade
   d. A Stake in the Outcome

2. In economics, _____ refers to the ability of a person or a country to produce a particular good at a lower marginal cost and opportunity cost than another person or country. It is the ability to produce a product most efficiently given all the other products that could be produced. It can be contrasted with absolute advantage which refers to the ability of a person or a country to produce a particular good at a lower absolute cost than another.
   a. Comparative advantage
   b. 33 Strategies of War
   c. 1990 Clean Air Act
   d. 28-hour day

3. The _____ is the difference between the monetary value of exports and imports of output in an economy over a certain period of time. It is the relationship between a nation's imports and exports. A favourable _____ is known as a trade surplus and consists of exporting more than is imported; an unfavourable _____ is known as a trade deficit or, informally, a trade gap.
   a. Value added
   b. Balance of trade
   c. Deregulation
   d. Minimum wage

4. _____ is a broad label that refers to any individuals or households that use goods and services generated within the economy. The concept of a _____ is used in different contexts, so that the usage and significance of the term may vary.

Typically when business people and economists talk of _____s they are talking about person as _____, an aggregated commodity item with little individuality other than that expressed in the buy/not-buy decision.

   a. Consumer
   b. 28-hour day
   c. 33 Strategies of War
   d. 1990 Clean Air Act

Chapter 6. International Business

5. _____ is a business management strategy aimed at embedding awareness of quality in all organizational processes. _____ has been widely used in manufacturing, education, hospitals, call centers, government, and service industries, as well as NASA space and science programs.

As defined by the International Organization for Standardization (ISO):

> '_____ is a management approach for an organization, centered on quality, based on the participation of all its members and aiming at long-term success through customer satisfaction, and benefits to all members of the organization and to society.' ISO 8402:1994

One major aim is to reduce variation from every process so that greater consistency of effort is obtained. (Royse, D., Thyer, B., Padgett D., ' Logan T., 2006)

   a. Quality management
   b. Total quality management
   c. 28-hour day
   d. 1990 Clean Air Act

6. _____, commonly known as e-commerce, consists of the buying and selling of products or services over electronic systems such as the Internet and other computer networks. The amount of trade conducted electronically has grown extraordinarily with widespread Internet usage. The use of commerce is conducted in this way, spurring and drawing on innovations in electronic funds transfer, supply chain management, Internet marketing, online transaction processing, electronic data interchange (EDI), inventory management systems, and automated data collection systems.
   a. Online shopping
   b. A Stake in the Outcome
   c. A4e
   d. Electronic Commerce

7. _____ is the branch of economics that studies the dynamics of exchange rates, foreign investment, and how these affect international trade. It also studies international projects, international investments and capital flows, and trade deficits. It includes the study of futures, options and currency swaps.
   a. AAAI
   b. A Stake in the Outcome
   c. A4e
   d. International finance

8. _____ can be regarded as an outcome of mental processes (cognitive process) leading to the selection of a course of action among several alternatives. Every _____ process produces a final choice. The output can be an action or an opinion of choice.

a. 33 Strategies of War
b. Decision making
c. 1990 Clean Air Act
d. 28-hour day

9. _____ is a type of trade policy that allows traders to act and transact without interference from government. Thus, the policy permits trading partners mutual gains from trade, with goods and services produced according to the theory of comparative advantage.

Under a _____ policy, prices are a reflection of true supply and demand, and are the sole determinant of resource allocation.

a. 33 Strategies of War
b. 1990 Clean Air Act
c. Free Trade
d. 28-hour day

10. _____ is a designated group of countries that have agreed to eliminate tariffs, quotas and preferences on most (if not all) goods and services traded between them. It can be considered the second stage of economic integration. Countries choose this kind of economic integration form if their economical structures are complementary.
a. 33 Strategies of War
b. 28-hour day
c. 1990 Clean Air Act
d. Free trade area

11. A _____ or labor union is an organization of workers who have banded together to achieve common goals in key areas and working conditions. The _____, through its leadership, bargains with the employer on behalf of union members (rank and file members) and negotiates labor contracts (Collective bargaining) with employers. This may include the negotiation of wages, work rules, complaint procedures, rules governing hiring, firing and promotion of workers, benefits, workplace safety and policies.
a. Trade union
b. Working time
c. Company union
d. Labour law

12. The _____ is a trilateral trade bloc in North America created by the governments of the United States, Canada, and Mexico. The agreement creating the trade bloc came into force on January 1, 1994. It superseded the Canada-United States Free Trade Agreement between the U.S. and Canada.

a. Trade union
b. North American Free Trade Agreement
c. Career portfolios
d. Business war game

13. A _____ or transnational corporation is a corporation or enterprise that manages production or delivers services in more than one country. It can also be referred to as an international corporation.

The first modern _____ is generally thought to be the Dutch East India Company, established in 1602.

a. Financial Accounting Standards Board
b. Multinational corporation
c. Command center
d. Small and medium enterprises

14. A _____ is a formal relationship between two or more parties to pursue a set of agreed upon goals or to meet a critical business need while remaining independent organizations.

Partners may provide the _____ with resources such as products, distribution channels, manufacturing capability, project funding, capital equipment, knowledge, expertise, or intellectual property. The alliance is a cooperation or collaboration which aims for a synergy where each partner hopes that the benefits from the alliance will be greater than those from individual efforts.

a. Golden parachute
b. Strategic alliance
c. Process automation
d. Farmshoring

15. A _____ is an alliance among individuals or groups, during which they cooperate in joint action, each in his own self-interest, joining forces together for a common cause. This alliance may be temporary or a matter of convenience. A _____ thus differs from a more formal covenant.

a. 28-hour day
b. 33 Strategies of War
c. 1990 Clean Air Act
d. Coalition

Chapter 7. The Basics of Planning and Strategic Management

1. A _____ is a plan devised for a specific situation when things could go wrong. _____s are often devised by governments or businesses who want to be prepared for anything that could happen. They are sometimes known as 'Back-up plans', 'Worst-case scenario plans' or 'Plan B'.
   a. 28-hour day
   b. 1990 Clean Air Act
   c. Contingency plan
   d. 33 Strategies of War

2. _____ is an area of business concerned with the production of goods and services, and involves the responsibility of ensuring that business operations are efficient in terms of using as little resource as needed, and effective in terms of meeting customer requirements. It is concerned with managing the process that converts inputs (in the forms of materials, labour and energy) into outputs (in the form of goods and services.)

   Operations traditionally refers to the production of goods and services separately, although the distinction between these two main types of operations is increasingly difficult to make as manufacturers tend to merge product and service offerings.

   a. A Stake in the Outcome
   b. A4e
   c. AAAI
   d. Operations management

3. _____ is an organization's process of defining its strategy and making decisions on allocating its resources to pursue this strategy, including its capital and people. Various business analysis techniques can be used in _____, including SWOT analysis (Strengths, Weaknesses, Opportunities, and Threats) and PEST analysis (Political, Economic, Social, and Technological analysis) or STEER analysis involving Socio-cultural, Technological, Economic, Ecological, and Regulatory factors and EPISTEL (Environment, Political, Informatic, Social, Technological, Economic and Legal)

   _____ is the formal consideration of an organization's future course. All _____ deals with at least one of three key questions:

   1. 'What do we do?'
   2. 'For whom do we do it?'
   3. 'How do we excel?'

   In business _____, the third question is better phrased 'How can we beat or avoid competition?'. (Bradford and Duncan, page 1.)

Chapter 7. The Basics of Planning and Strategic Management

a. 33 Strategies of War
b. Strategic planning
c. 1990 Clean Air Act
d. 28-hour day

4. _____ is one of the managerial functions like planning, organizing, staffing and directing. It is an important function because it helps to check the errors and to take the corrective action so that deviation from standards are minimized and stated goals of the organization are achieved in desired manner. According to modern concepts, _____ is a foreseeing action whereas earlier concept of _____ was used only when errors were detected. _____ in management means setting standards, measuring actual performance and taking corrective action.
   a. Control
   b. Schedule of reinforcement
   c. Turnover
   d. Decision tree pruning

5. _____ is a process of agreeing upon objectives within an organization so that management and employees agree to the objectives and understand what they are in the organization.

The term '_____' was first popularized by Peter Drucker in his 1954 book 'The Practice of Management'.

The essence of _____ is participative goal setting, choosing course of actions and decision making.

   a. Management by objectives
   b. Business economics
   c. Job enrichment
   d. Clean sheet review

6. In finance and economics, _____ or divestiture is the reduction of some kind of asset for either financial or ethical objectives or sale of an existing business by a firm. A _____ is the opposite of an investment.
   a. 28-hour day
   b. 1990 Clean Air Act
   c. 33 Strategies of War
   d. Divestment

Chapter 7. The Basics of Planning and Strategic Management

7. In law, _____ refers to the process by which a company (or part of a company) is brought to an end, and the assets and property of the company redistributed. _____ can also be referred to as winding-up or dissolution, although dissolution technically refers to the last stage of _____. The process of _____ also arises when customs, an authority or agency in a country responsible for collecting and safeguarding customs duties, determines the final computation or ascertainment of the duties or drawback accruing on an entry.

   a. Liquidation
   b. 1990 Clean Air Act
   c. 33 Strategies of War
   d. 28-hour day

8. In economics, business, retail, and accounting, a _____ is the value of money that has been used up to produce something, and hence is not available for use anymore. In economics, a _____ is an alternative that is given up as a result of a decision. In business, the _____ may be one of acquisition, in which case the amount of money expended to acquire it is counted as _____.

   a. Cost allocation
   b. Fixed costs
   c. Cost overrun
   d. Cost

9. _____ is a concept developed by Michael Porter, used in business strategy. It describes a way to establish the competitive advantage. _____, in basic words, means the lowest cost of operation in the industry.

   a. Switching cost
   b. Strategic group
   c. Cost leadership
   d. Strategic business unit

10. _____ has been described as the 'process of social influence in which one person can enlist the aid and support of others in the accomplishment of a common task'. A definition more inclusive of followers comes from Alan Keith of Genentech who said '_____ is ultimately about creating a way for people to contribute to making something extraordinary happen.'

    _____ is one of the most salient aspects of the organizational context. However, defining _____ has been challenging.

   a. Situational leadership
   b. 1990 Clean Air Act
   c. 28-hour day
   d. Leadership

Chapter 7. The Basics of Planning and Strategic Management

11. _____ is a process of planning and controlling the performance or execution of any type of activity, such as:

- a project (project _____) or
- a process (process _____, sometimes referred to as the process performance measurement and management system.)

Organization's senior management is responsible for carrying out its _____.

a. Management process
b. Participatory management
c. Human Relations Movement
d. Work design

12. _____ is a strategic planning method used to evaluate the Strengths, Weaknesses, Opportunities, and Threats involved in a project or in a business venture. It involves specifying the objective of the business venture or project and identifying the internal and external factors that are favorable and unfavorable to achieving that objective. The technique is credited to Albert Humphrey, who led a convention at Stanford University in the 1960s and 1970s using data from Fortune 500 companies.

a. Corporate image
b. Market share
c. SWOT analysis
d. Marketing

Chapter 8. Organizing Work

1. _____ is the process by which the activities of an organisation, particularly those regarding decision-making, become concentrated within a particular location and/or group.
   a. Chief operating officer
   b. Corner office
   c. Product innovation
   d. Centralization

2. _____ is the process of dispersing decision-making governance closer to the people or citizen. It includes the dispersal of administration or governance in sectors or areas like engineering, management science, political science, political economy, sociology and economics. _____ is also possible in the dispersal of population and employment.
   a. Business plan
   b. Formula for Change
   c. Frenemy
   d. Decentralization

3. The _____ is the interlocking social structure that governs how people work together in practice. It is the aggregate of behaviors, interactions, norms, personal and professional connections through which work gets done and relationships are built among people who share a common organizational affiliation or cluster of affiliations. It consists of a dynamic set of personal relationships, social networks, communities of common interest, and emotional sources of motivation. The _____ evolves organically and spontaneously in response to changes in the work environment, the flux of people through its porous boundaries, and the complex social dynamics of its members.
   a. Organizational effectiveness
   b. Union shop
   c. Open shop
   d. Informal organization

4. _____ describes the situation when output from (or information about the result of) an event or phenomenon in the past will influence the same event/phenomenon in the present or future. When an event is part of a chain of cause-and-effect that forms a circuit or loop, then the event is said to 'feed back' into itself.

   _____ is also a synonym for:

   - _____ signal; the information about the initial event that is the basis for subsequent modification of the event.
   - _____ loop; the causal path that leads from the initial generation of the _____ signal to the subsequent modification of the event.

   _____ is a mechanism, process or signal that is looped back to control a system within itself. Such a loop is called a _____ loop.

a. Positive feedback
b. Feedback loop
c. 1990 Clean Air Act
d. Feedback

5. In a military context, the _____ is the line of authority and responsibility along which orders are passed within a military unit and between different units. The term is also used in a civilian management context describing comparable hierarchical structures of authority.
   a. 1990 Clean Air Act
   b. 28-hour day
   c. French leave
   d. Chain of command

6. _____ is a 'policy by which management devotes its time to investigating only those situations in which actual results differ significantly from planned results. The idea is that management should spend its valuable time concentrating on the more important items (such as shaping the company's future strategic course.) Attention is given only to material deviations requiring investigation.'

   It is not entirely synonymous with the concept of exception management in that it describes a policy where absolute focus is on exception management, in contrast to moderate application of exception management.

   a. C-A-K-E
   b. Business philosophy
   c. Management by exception
   d. Trustee

7. The _____ is a standardized, on-scene, all-hazard incident management concept. It is a management protocol originally designed for emergency management agencies in the United States which was later federalized there. It has since been adopted by agencies in other countries.
   a. A Stake in the Outcome
   b. AAAI
   c. A4e
   d. Incident Command Structure

8. _____ is a term originating in military organization theory, but now used more commonly in business management, particularly human resource management. _____ refers to the number of subordinates a supervisor has.

Chapter 8. Organizing Work

In the hierarchical business organization of the past it was not uncommon to see average spans of 1 to 10 or even less. That is, one manager supervised ten employees on average.

- a. CIFMS
- b. Span of control
- c. Mentoring
- d. Senior management

9. _____ is one of the managerial functions like planning, organizing, staffing and directing. It is an important function because it helps to check the errors and to take the corrective action so that deviation from standards are minimized and stated goals of the organization are achieved in desired manner. According to modern concepts, _____ is a foreseeing action whereas earlier concept of _____ was used only when errors were detected. _____ in management means setting standards, measuring actual performance and taking corrective action.

- a. Schedule of reinforcement
- b. Turnover
- c. Decision tree pruning
- d. Control

10. _____ refers to increasing the spiritual, political, social or economic strength of individuals and communities. It often involves the empowered developing confidence in their own capacities.

The term Human _____ covers a vast landscape of meanings, interpretations, definitions and disciplines ranging from psychology and philosophy to the highly commercialized Self-Help industry and Motivational sciences.

- a. Empowerment
- b. A4e
- c. A Stake in the Outcome
- d. AAAI

11. _____ is a variable work schedule, in contrast to traditional work arrangements requiring employees to work a standard 9am to 5pm day. Under _____, there is typically a core period of the day when employees are expected to be at work (for example, between 11 am and 3pm), while the rest of the working day is 'flexitime', in which employees can choose when they work, subject to achieving total daily, weekly or monthly hours in the region of what the employer expects, and subject to the necessary work being done.

A _____ policy allows staff to determine when they will work, while a flexplace policy allows staff to determine where they will work.

Chapter 8. Organizing Work

a. Certificate of Incorporation
b. Fiduciary
c. Flextime
d. Bennett Amendment

12. _____, e-commuting, e-work, telework, working from home (WFH), or working at home (WAH) is a work arrangement in which employees enjoy flexibility in working location and hours. In other words, the daily commute to a central place of work is replaced by telecommunication links. Many work from home, while others, occasionally also referred to as nomad workers or web commuters utilize mobile telecommunications technology to work from coffee shops or myriad other locations.
    a. 28-hour day
    b. 33 Strategies of War
    c. 1990 Clean Air Act
    d. Telecommuting

13. _____ can be regarded as an outcome of mental processes (cognitive process) leading to the selection of a course of action among several alternatives. Every _____ process produces a final choice. The output can be an action or an opinion of choice.
    a. 1990 Clean Air Act
    b. 28-hour day
    c. 33 Strategies of War
    d. Decision making

Chapter 9. Organizational Structure

1. An _____, or organogram(me)) is a diagram that shows the structure of an organization and the relationships and relative ranks of its parts and positions/jobs. The term is also used for similar diagrams, for example ones showing the different elements of a field of knowledge or a group of languages. The French Encyclopédie had one of the first _____s of knowledge in general.
   a. A4e
   b. Organizational chart
   c. AAAI
   d. A Stake in the Outcome

2. _____ can be regarded as an outcome of mental processes (cognitive process) leading to the selection of a course of action among several alternatives. Every _____ process produces a final choice. The output can be an action or an opinion of choice.
   a. Decision making
   b. 28-hour day
   c. 1990 Clean Air Act
   d. 33 Strategies of War

3. An _____ is a mostly hierarchical concept of subordination of entities that collaborate and contribute to serve one common aim.

   Organizations are a variant of clustered entities. The structure of an organization is usually set up in many a styles, dependent on their objectives and ambience.

   a. Open shop
   b. Organizational development
   c. Informal organization
   d. Organizational structure

4. _____ is subcontracting a process, such as product design or manufacturing, to a third-party company. The decision to outsource is often made in the interest of lowering cost or making better use of time and energy costs, redirecting or conserving energy directed at the competencies of a particular business, or to make more efficient use of land, labor, capital, (information) technology and resources. _____ became part of the business lexicon during the 1980s.
   a. Unemployment insurance
   b. Outsourcing
   c. Operant conditioning
   d. Opinion leadership

5. _____ refers to the process of grouping activities into departments.

Chapter 9. Organizational Structure

Division of labour creates specialists who need coordination. This coordination is facilitated by grouping specialists together in departments.

a. Maximum wage
b. Departmentalization
c. Division of labour
d. Decent work

6. A _____ is a list of the general tasks and responsibilities of a position. Typically, it also includes to whom the position reports, specifications such as the qualifications needed by the person in the job, salary range for the position, etc. A _____ is usually developed by conducting a job analysis, which includes examining the tasks and sequences of tasks necessary to perform the job.
  a. Recruitment
  b. Recruitment Process Insourcing
  c. Recruitment advertising
  d. Job description

7. _____ refers to the movement of cash into or out of a business or financial product. It is usually measured during a specified, finite period of time. Measurement of _____ can be used

   - to determine a project's rate of return or value. The time of _____s into and out of projects are used as inputs in financial models such as internal rate of return, and net present value.
   - to determine problems with a business's liquidity. Being profitable does not necessarily mean being liquid. A company can fail because of a shortage of cash, even while profitable.
   - as an alternate measure of a business's profits when it is believed that accrual accounting concepts do not represent economic realities. For example, a company may be notionally profitable but generating little operational cash (as may be the case for a company that barters its products rather than selling for cash.) In such a case, the company may be deriving additional operating cash by issuing shares evaluating default risk, re-investment requirements, etc.

   _____ is a generic term used differently depending on the context. It may be defined by users for their own purposes.

   a. Gross profit
   b. Sweat equity
   c. Gross profit margin
   d. Cash flow

8. The term '_____' refers to the concept of collecting information and attempting to spot a pattern in the information. In some fields of study, the term '_____' has more formally-defined meanings.

In project management _____ is a mathematical technique that uses historical results to predict future outcome.

   a. Regression analysis
   b. Least squares
   c. Trend analysis
   d. Stepwise regression

9. A _____ is a body of elected or appointed members who jointly oversee the activities of a company or organization. The body sometimes has a different name, such as board of trustees, board of governors, board of managers, or executive board. It is often simply referred to as 'the board.'

A board's activities are determined by the powers, duties, and responsibilities delegated to it or conferred on it by an authority outside itself.

   a. Competition law
   b. Board of directors
   c. Foreign Corrupt Practices Act
   d. Clean Water Act

Chapter 10. Understanding Work Groups and Teams

1. _____ is a type of thought exhibited by group members who try to minimize conflict and reach consensus without critically testing, analyzing, and evaluating ideas. Individual creativity, uniqueness, and independent thinking are lost in the pursuit of group cohesiveness, as are the advantages of reasonable balance in choice and thought that might normally be obtained by making decisions as a group. During _____, members of the group avoid promoting viewpoints outside the comfort zone of consensus thinking.
   a. Groupthink
   b. Diffusion of responsibility
   c. Self-report inventory
   d. Psychological statistics

2. The _____ is a form of reactivity whereby subjects improve an aspect of their behavior being experimentally measured simply in response to the fact that they are being studied, not in response to any particular experimental manipulation.

   The term was coined in 1955 by Henry A. Landsberger when analyzing older experiments from 1924-1932 at the Hawthorne Works (outside Chicago.) Hawthorne Works had commissioned a study to see if its workers would become more productive in higher or lower levels of light.

   a. 28-hour day
   b. 33 Strategies of War
   c. 1990 Clean Air Act
   d. Hawthorne effect

3. The _____ is given by the United States National Institute of Standards and Technology. Through the actions of the National Productivity Advisory Committee chaired by Jack Grayson, it was established by the Malcolm Baldrige National Quality Improvement Act of 1987 - Public Law 100-107 and named for Malcolm Baldrige, who served as United States Secretary of Commerce during the Reagan administration from 1981 until his 1987 death in a rodeo accident. APQC, , organized the first White House Conference on Productivity, spearheading the creation and design of the _____ in 1987, and jointly administering the award for its first three years.
   a. Time and attendance
   b. Scenario planning
   c. Business Network Transformation
   d. Malcolm Baldrige National Quality Award

4. A _____ is a volunteer group composed of workers (or even students), usually under the leadership of their supervisor (but they can elect a team leader), who are trained to identify, analyse and solve work-related problems and present their solutions to management in order to improve the performance of the organization, and motivate and enrich the work of employees. When matured, true _____s become self-managing, having gained the confidence of management.
   _____s are an alternative to the dehumanising concept of the Division of Labour, where workers or individuals are treated like robots.

a. Competency-based job descriptions
b. Certified in Production and Inventory Management
c. Connectionist expert systems
d. Quality circle

5. _____ refers to metrics and measures of output from production processes, per unit of input. Labor _____, for example, is typically measured as a ratio of output per labor-hour, an input. _____ may be conceived of as a metrics of the technical or engineering efficiency of production.
   a. Master production schedule
   b. Productivity
   c. Value engineering
   d. Remanufacturing

6. A _____ -- also known as a geographically dispersed team -- is a group of individuals who work across time, space, and organizational boundaries with links strengthened by webs of communication technology. They have complementary skills and are committed to a common purpose, have interdependent performance goals, and share an approach to work for which they hold themselves mutually accountable. Geographically dispersed teams allow organizations to hire and retain the best people regardless of location.
   a. Trademark
   b. Virtual Team
   c. Risk management
   d. Kanban

Chapter 11. Staffing

1. _____ is subcontracting a process, such as product design or manufacturing, to a third-party company. The decision to outsource is often made in the interest of lowering cost or making better use of time and energy costs, redirecting or conserving energy directed at the competencies of a particular business, or to make more efficient use of land, labor, capital, (information) technology and resources. _____ became part of the business lexicon during the 1980s.

   a. Unemployment insurance
   b. Operant conditioning
   c. Outsourcing
   d. Opinion leadership

2. Organizational culture is not the same as _____. It is wider and deeper concepts, something that an organization 'is' rather than what it 'has' (according to Buchanan and Huczynski.)

   _____ is the total sum of the values, customs, traditions and meanings that make a company unique.

   a. Path-goal theory
   b. Corporate culture
   c. Job analysis
   d. Work design

3. In the field of human resource management, _____ is the field concerned with organizational activity aimed at bettering the performance of individuals and groups in organizational settings. It has been known by several names, including employee development, human resource development, and learning and development.

   Harrison observes that the name was endlessly debated by the Chartered Institute of Personnel and Development during its review of professional standards in 1999/2000.

   a. Person specification
   b. Revolving door syndrome
   c. Training and development
   d. Performance appraisal

4. _____ refers to various methodologies for analyzing the requirements of a job.

   The general purpose of _____ is to document the requirements of a job and the work performed. Job and task analysis is performed as a basis for later improvements, including: definition of a job domain; describing a job; developing performance appraisals, selection systems, promotion criteria, training needs assessment, and compensation plans.

a. Hersey-Blanchard situational theory
b. Work design
c. Job analysis
d. Management process

5. A _____ is a list of the general tasks and responsibilities of a position. Typically, it also includes to whom the position reports, specifications such as the qualifications needed by the person in the job, salary range for the position, etc. A _____ is usually developed by conducting a job analysis, which includes examining the tasks and sequences of tasks necessary to perform the job.
  a. Recruitment
  b. Recruitment Process Insourcing
  c. Job description
  d. Recruitment advertising

6. _____ is the process of estimation in unknown situations. Prediction is a similar, but more general term. Both can refer to estimation of time series, cross-sectional or longitudinal data.
  a. 33 Strategies of War
  b. 28-hour day
  c. 1990 Clean Air Act
  d. Forecasting

7. _____ is an increasingly broadening term with which an organization, or other human system describes the combination of traditionally administrative personnel functions with acquisition and application of skills, knowledge and experience, Employee Relations and resource planning at various levels. The field draws upon concepts developed in Industrial/Organizational Psychology and System Theory. _____ has at least two related interpretations depending on context. The original usage derives from political economy and economics, where it was traditionally called labor, one of four factors of production although this perspective is changing as a function of new and ongoing research into more strategic approaches at national levels. This first usage is used more in terms of '_____ development', and can go beyond just organizations to the level of nations . The more traditional usage within corporations and businesses refers to the individuals within a firm or agency, and to the portion of the organization that deals with hiring, firing, training, and other personnel issues, typically referred to as `_____ management'.
  a. Human resource management
  b. Bradford Factor
  c. Progressive discipline
  d. Human resources

8. The _____ was a landmark piece of legislation in the United States that outlawed racial segregation in schools, public places, and employment.

Chapter 11. Staffing

a. Design patent
b. Negligence in employment
c. Financial Security Law of France
d. Civil Rights Act of 1964

9. The _____ 1970 is an Act of the United Kingdom Parliament which prohibits any less favourable treatment between men and women in terms of pay and conditions of employment. It came into force on 29 December 1975. The term pay is interpreted in a broad sense to include, on top of wages, things like holidays, pension rights, company perks and some kinds of bonuses.

  a. Oncale v. Sundowner Offshore Services
  b. Architectural Barriers Act of 1968
  c. Australian labour law
  d. Equal Pay Act

10. The _____, Pub. L. No. 88-38, 77 Stat. 56, (June 10, 1963) codified at 29 U.S.C. § 206(d), is a United States federal law amending the Fair Labor Standards Act, aimed at abolishing wage differentials based on sex. In passing the bill, Congress denounces sex discrimination.

  a. Extra time
  b. Architectural Barriers Act of 1968
  c. Invitee
  d. Equal Pay Act of 1963

11. The term _____ was created by President Lyndon B. Johnson when he signed Executive Order 11246 on September 24, 1965, created to prohibit federal contractors from discriminating against employees on the basis of race, sex, creed, religion, color, or national origin. In more recent times, most employers have also added sexual orientation to the list of non-discrimination.

The Executive Order also required contractors to implement affirmative action plans to increase the participation of minorities and women in the workplace.

  a. Equal employment opportunity
  b. A Stake in the Outcome
  c. A4e
  d. AAAI

Chapter 11. Staffing

12. _____ is a contract between two parties, one being the employer and the other being the employee. An employee may be defined as: 'A person in the service of another under any contract of hire, express or implied, oral or written, where the employer has the power or right to control and direct the employee in the material details of how the work is to be performed.' Black's Law Dictionary page 471 (5th ed. 1979.)

    a. Employment rate
    b. Exit interview
    c. Employment counsellor
    d. Employment

13. The _____ of 1967, Pub. L. No. 90-202, 81 Stat. 602 (Dec. 15, 1967), codified as Chapter 14 of Title 29 of the United States Code, 29 U.S.C. § 621 through 29 U.S.C. § 634 (ADEA), prohibits employment discrimination against persons 40 years of age or older in the United States). The law also sets standards for pensions and benefits provided by employers and requires that information about the needs of older workers be provided to the general public.

    a. Extra time
    b. Undue hardship
    c. Unemployment and Farm Relief Act
    d. Age Discrimination in Employment Act

14. The _____ is a United States statute that was passed in response to a series of United States Supreme Court decisions which limited the rights of employees who had sued their employers for discrimination. The Act represented the first effort since the passage of the Civil Rights Act of 1964 to modify some of the basic procedural and substantive rights provided by federal law in employment discrimination cases. It provided for the right to trial by jury on discrimination claims and introduced the possibility of emotional distress damages, while limiting the amount that a jury could award

The 1991 Act combined elements from two different civil rights acts of the past: the Civil Rights Act of 1866, better known by the number assigned to it in the codification of federal laws as 'Section 1981', and the employment-related provisions of the Civil Rights Act of 1964, generally referred to as 'Title VII', its location within the Act.

    a. Negligence in employment
    b. Resource Conservation and Recovery Act
    c. Covenant
    d. Civil Rights Act of 1991

15. The _____ is a United States labor law allowing an employee to take unpaid leave due to a serious health condition that makes the employee unable to perform his job or to care for a sick family member or to care for a new son or daughter (including by birth, adoption or foster care.) The bill was among the first signed into law by President Bill Clinton in his first term.

Chapter 11. Staffing

a. Contributory negligence
b. Sarbanes-Oxley Act of 2002
c. Harvester Judgment
d. Family and Medical Leave Act of 1993

16. The U.S. _____ of 1973 prohibits discrimination on the basis of disability in programs conducted by Federal agencies, in programs receiving Federal financial assistance, in Federal employment, and in the employment practices of Federal contractors. The standards for determining employment discrimination under the _____ are the same as those used in title I of the Americans with Disabilities Act.

There are four key sections of the Act.

a. 1990 Clean Air Act
b. 33 Strategies of War
c. 28-hour day
d. Rehabilitation Act

17. _____ is one of the managerial functions like planning, organizing, staffing and directing. It is an important function because it helps to check the errors and to take the corrective action so that deviation from standards are minimized and stated goals of the organization are achieved in desired manner. According to modern concepts, _____ is a foreseeing action whereas earlier concept of _____ was used only when errors were detected. _____ in management means setting standards, measuring actual performance and taking corrective action.

a. Turnover
b. Control
c. Schedule of reinforcement
d. Decision tree pruning

18. _____ occurs when expectant women are fired, not hired, or otherwise discriminated against due to their pregnancy or intention to become pregnant. Common forms of _____ include not being hired due to visible pregnancy or likelihood of becoming pregnant, being fired after informing an employer of one's pregnancy, being fired after maternity leave, and receiving a pay dock due to pregnancy. In the United States, since 1978, employers are legally bound to provide what insurance, leave pay, and additional support that would be bestowed upon any employee with medical leave or disability.

a. 1990 Clean Air Act
b. 28-hour day
c. 33 Strategies of War
d. Pregnancy Discrimination

19. The _____ is the principle that 'In a Hierarchy Every Employee Tends to Rise to His Level of Incompetence.' While formulated by Dr. Laurence J. Peter and Raymond Hull in their 1968 book The _____, a humorous treatise which also introduced the 'salutary science of Hierarchiology', 'inadvertently founded' by Peter, the principle has real validity. It holds that in a hierarchy, members are promoted so long as they work competently. Sooner or later they are promoted to a position at which they are no longer competent (their 'level of incompetence'), and there they remain, being unable to earn further promotions.

   a. Democracy in America
   b. BusinessWeek
   c. Waiting for the Weekend
   d. Peter Principle

20. _____ refers to the process of screening, and selecting qualified people for a job at an organization or firm mid- and large-size organizations and companies often retain professional recruiters or outsource some of the process to _____ agencies. External _____ is the process of attracting and selecting employees from outside the organization.

The _____ industry has four main types of agencies: employment agencies, _____ websites and job search engines, 'headhunters' for executive and professional _____, and in-house _____.

   a. Labour hire
   b. Referral recruitment
   c. Recruitment
   d. Recruitment Process Outsourcing

21.

The terms _____ and positive action refer to policies that take race, ethnicity, or gender into consideration in an attempt to promote equal opportunity. The focus of such policies ranges from employment and education to public contracting and health programs. The impetus towards _____ is twofold: to maximize diversity in all levels of society, along with its presumed benefits, and to redress perceived disadvantages due to overt, institutional, or involuntary discrimination.

   a. Abraham Harold Maslow
   b. Adam Smith
   c. Affiliation
   d. Affirmative action

22. _____ can be regarded as an outcome of mental processes (cognitive process) leading to the selection of a course of action among several alternatives. Every _____ process produces a final choice. The output can be an action or an opinion of choice.

Chapter 11. Staffing

a. 1990 Clean Air Act
b. 33 Strategies of War
c. 28-hour day
d. Decision making

23. _____ is, in its simplest form, the practice of favoring members of a historically disadvantaged group at the expense of members of a historically advantaged group.

In the United States, the terms '_____' and 'reverse racism' have been used in past discussions of racial quotas or gender quotas for collegiate admission to government-run educational institutions. Such policies were held to be unconstitutional in the United States, while non-quota race preferences are legal.

a. Separate but equal
b. Reverse discrimination
c. 1990 Clean Air Act
d. Sexism,

24. _____ measures one's mastery of the concepts needed to perform certain work.

_____ is a complex concept that includes elements of both ability (capacity to learn) and seniority (opportunity to learn.) It is usually measured with a paper-and-pencil test.

a. Performance appraisal
b. Personnel management
c. Job knowledge
d. Revolving door syndrome

25. The term _____ in logic applies to arguments or statements.

An argument is valid if and only if the truth of its premises entails the truth of its conclusion, it would be self-contradictory to affirm the premises and deny the conclusion. The corresponding conditional of a valid argument is a logical truth and the negation of its corresponding conditional is a contradiction.

a. 1990 Clean Air Act
b. Simplification
c. Validity
d. Fuzzy logic

Chapter 11. Staffing

26. The U.S. _____ of 1988 ('_____') generally prevents employers from using lie detector tests, either for pre-employment screening or during the course of employment, with certain exemptions. Employers generally may not require or request any employee or job applicant to take a lie detector test, or discharge, discipline, or discriminate against an employee or job applicant for refusing to take a test or for exercising other rights under the Act. In addition, employers are required to display a poster in the workplace explaining the _____ for their employees.

   a. A Stake in the Outcome
   b. AAAI
   c. Employee Polygraph Protection Act
   d. A4e

27. A _____ or background investigation is the process of looking up and compiling criminal records, commercial records and financial records (in certain instances such as employment screening) of an individual.

   _____s are often requested by employers on job candidates, especially on candidates seeking a position that requires high security or a position of trust, such as in a school, hospital, financial institution, airport, and government (including law enforcement and military.) These checks are traditionally administered by a government agency for a nominal fee, but can also be administered by private companies.

   a. Malcolm Baldrige National Quality Award
   b. Time and attendance
   c. Background check
   d. Labour productivity

28. A _____ is a process in which a potential employee is evaluated by an employer for prospective employment in their company, organization and was established in the late 16th century.

   A _____ typically precedes the hiring decision, and is used to evaluate the candidate. The interview is usually preceded by the evaluation of submitted résumés from interested candidates, then selecting a small number of candidates for interviews.

   a. Supported employment
   b. Payrolling
   c. Split shift
   d. Job interview

29. A _____ is a quantitative research method commonly employed in survey research. The aim of this approach is to ensure that each interviewee is presented with exactly the same questions in the same order. This ensures that answers can be reliably aggregated and that comparisons can be made with confidence between sample subgroups or between different survey periods.

a. Questionnaire
b. Mystery shoppers
c. Questionnaire construction
d. Structured interview

30. _____ are a method of interviews where questions can be changed or adapted to meet the respondent's intelligence, understanding or belief. Unlike a structured interview they do not offer a limited, pre-set range of answers for a respondent to choose, but instead advocate listening to how each individual person responds to the question.

The method to gather information using this technique is fairly limited, for example most surveys that are carried out via telephone or even in person tend to follow a structured method.

a. A4e
b. AAAI
c. A Stake in the Outcome
d. Unstructured interviews

31. The _____ refers to a cognitive bias whereby the perception of a particular trait is influenced by the perception of the former traits in a sequence of interpretations.

Edward L. Thorndike was the first to support the _____ with empirical research. In a psychology study published in 1920, Thorndike asked commanding officers to rate their soldiers; Thorndike found high cross-correlation between all positive and all negative traits.

a. Distinction bias
b. Cognitive biases
c. Sunk costs
d. Halo effect

32. _____ is the harmful physical and emotional response that occurs when there is a poor match between job demands and the capabilities, resources, or needs of the worker.

Stress-related disorders encompass a broad array of conditions, including psychological disorders (e.g. depression, anxiety, post-traumatic stress disorder) and other types of emotional strain (e.g., dissatisfaction, fatigue, tension, etc.), maladaptive behaviors (e.g., aggression, substance abuse), and cognitive impairment (e.g., concentration and memory problems.) In turn, these conditions may lead to poor work performance or even injury.

a. Workplace stress
b. 33 Strategies of War
c. 1990 Clean Air Act
d. 28-hour day

Chapter 12. Employee Training and Development

1. In the field of human resource management, _____ is the field concerned with organizational activity aimed at bettering the performance of individuals and groups in organizational settings. It has been known by several names, including employee development, human resource development, and learning and development.

    Harrison observes that the name was endlessly debated by the Chartered Institute of Personnel and Development during its review of professional standards in 1999/2000.

    a. Training and development
    b. Person specification
    c. Revolving door syndrome
    d. Performance appraisal

2. In business and accounting, _____s are everything of value that is owned by a person or company. Any property or object of value that one possesses, usually considered as applicable to the payment of one's debts is considered an _____. Simplistically stated, _____s are things of value that can be readily converted into cash.

    a. A4e
    b. AAAI
    c. Asset
    d. A Stake in the Outcome

3. _____ is a process for determining and addressing needs, or gaps between current conditions and desired conditions organizations it is known as community needs analysis. It involves identifying material problems/deficits/weaknesses and advantages/opportunites/strengths, and evaluating possible solutions that take those qualities into consideration.

    a. 33 Strategies of War
    b. 28-hour day
    c. 1990 Clean Air Act
    d. Needs assessment

4. _____ is a system of training a new generation of practitioners of a skill. Apprentices (or in early modern usage 'prentices') or prot>ég>és build their careers from _____s. Most of their training is done on the job while working for an employer who helps the apprentices learn their trade, in exchange for their continuing labour for an agreed period after they become skilled.

    a. A4e
    b. A Stake in the Outcome
    c. AAAI
    d. Apprenticeship

Chapter 12. Employee Training and Development

5. _____ refers to training in different ways to improve overall performance. It takes advantage of the particular effectiveness of each training method, while at the same time attempting to neglect the shortcomings of that method by combining it with other methods that address its weaknesses.

Cross training is employee-employer field means, training employees to do one another's work.

   a. 1990 Clean Air Act
   b. 28-hour day
   c. 33 Strategies of War
   d. Cross-training

6. _____ is an approach to management development where an individual is moved through a schedule of assignments designed to give him or her a breadth of exposure to the entire operation.

_____ is also practiced to allow qualified employees to gain more insights into the processes of a company, and to reduce boredom and increase job satisfaction through job variation.

The term _____ can also mean the scheduled exchange of persons in offices, especially in public offices, prior to the end of incumbency or the legislative period.

   a. 28-hour day
   b. Job rotation
   c. 33 Strategies of War
   d. 1990 Clean Air Act

7. _____ has been described as the 'process of social influence in which one person can enlist the aid and support of others in the accomplishment of a common task' . A definition more inclusive of followers comes from Alan Keith of Genentech who said '_____ is ultimately about creating a way for people to contribute to making something extraordinary happen.'

_____ is one of the most salient aspects of the organizational context. However, defining _____ has been challenging.

   a. Situational leadership
   b. Leadership
   c. 28-hour day
   d. 1990 Clean Air Act

8. _____ is best described as the process from which managers learn and improve their skills not only to benefit themselves but also their employing organizations.

Chapter 12. Employee Training and Development

In organisational development (OD), the effectiveness of management is recognised as one of the determinants of organisational success. Therefore, investment in _____ can have a direct economic benefit to the organization.

a. Job enrichment
b. Fix it twice
c. Senior management
d. Management development

9. _____ refers to the movement of cash into or out of a business or financial product. It is usually measured during a specified, finite period of time. Measurement of _____ can be used

- to determine a project's rate of return or value. The time of _____s into and out of projects are used as inputs in financial models such as internal rate of return, and net present value.
- to determine problems with a business's liquidity. Being profitable does not necessarily mean being liquid. A company can fail because of a shortage of cash, even while profitable.
- as an alternate measure of a business's profits when it is believed that accrual accounting concepts do not represent economic realities. For example, a company may be notionally profitable but generating little operational cash (as may be the case for a company that barters its products rather than selling for cash.) In such a case, the company may be deriving additional operating cash by issuing shares evaluating default risk, re-investment requirements, etc.

_____ is a generic term used differently depending on the context. It may be defined by users for their own purposes.

a. Sweat equity
b. Gross profit margin
c. Gross profit
d. Cash flow

Chapter 13. Motivating Employees

1. _____ is one of the managerial functions like planning, organizing, staffing and directing. It is an important function because it helps to check the errors and to take the corrective action so that deviation from standards are minimized and stated goals of the organization are achieved in desired manner. According to modern concepts, _____ is a foreseeing action whereas earlier concept of _____ was used only when errors were detected. _____ in management means setting standards, measuring actual performance and taking corrective action.

    a. Decision tree pruning
    b. Turnover
    c. Schedule of reinforcement
    d. Control

2. _____ attempts to explain relational satisfaction in terms of perceptions of fair/unfair distributions of resources within interpersonal relationships. _____ is considered as one of the justice theories, It was first developed in 1962 by John Stacey Adams, a workplace and behavioral psychologist, who asserted that employees seek to maintain equity between the inputs that they bring to a job and the outcomes that they receive from it against the perceived inputs and outcomes of others (Adams, 1965.) The belief is that people value fair treatment which causes them to be motivated to keep the fairness maintained within the relationships of their co-workers and the organization.

    a. A4e
    b. AAAI
    c. Equity theory
    d. A Stake in the Outcome

3. _____ has been described as the 'process of social influence in which one person can enlist the aid and support of others in the accomplishment of a common task' . A definition more inclusive of followers comes from Alan Keith of Genentech who said '_____ is ultimately about creating a way for people to contribute to making something extraordinary happen.'

    _____ is one of the most salient aspects of the organizational context. However, defining _____ has been challenging.

    a. Situational leadership
    b. 28-hour day
    c. 1990 Clean Air Act
    d. Leadership

4. _____ is a theory of management that analyzes and synthesizes workflows, with the objective of improving labour productivity. The core ideas of the theory were developed by Frederick Winslow Taylor in the 1880s and 1890s, and were first published in his monographs, Shop Management and The Principles of _____ Taylor believed that decisions based upon tradition and rules of thumb should be replaced by precise procedures developed after careful study of an individual at work.

a. Value engineering
b. Capacity planning
c. Master production schedule
d. Scientific management

5. Maslow's _____ is a theory in psychology, proposed by Abraham Maslow in his 1943 paper A Theory of Human Motivation, which he subsequently extended to include his observations of humans' innate curiosity.

Maslow's _____ is predetermined in order of importance. It is often depicted as a pyramid consisting of five levels: the lowest level is associated with physiological needs, while the uppermost level is associated with self-actualization needs, particularly those related to identity and purpose. Deficiency needs must be met first. Once these are met, seeking to satisfy growth needs drives personal growth. The higher needs in this hierarchy only come into focus when the lower needs in the pyramid are met.

a. 33 Strategies of War
b. 28-hour day
c. 1990 Clean Air Act
d. Hierarchy of needs

6. In law, _____ is the term to describe a partnership between two or more parties.

In England a number of statutes on the subject have been passed, the chief being the Bastardy Act of 1845, and the Bastardy Laws Amendment Acts of 1872 and 1873. The mother of a bastard may summon the putative father to petty sessions within twelve months of the birth (or at any later time if he is proved to have contributed to the child's support within twelve months after the birth), and the justices, as after hearing evidence on both sides, may, if the mother's evidence be corroborated in some material particular, adjudge the man to be the putative father of the child, and order him to pay a sum not exceeding five shillings a week for its maintenance, together with a sum for expenses incidental to the birth, or the funeral expenses, if it has died before the date of order, and the costs of the proceedings.

a. Adam Smith
b. Abraham Harold Maslow
c. Affirmative action
d. Affiliation

7. _____ means increasing the scope of a job through extending the range of its job duties and responsibilities. This contradicts the principles of specialisation and the division of labour whereby work is divided into small units, each of which is performed repetitively by an individual worker. Some motivational theories suggest that the boredom and alienation caused by the division of labour can actually cause efficiency to fall.

Chapter 13. Motivating Employees

a. Mock interview
b. Centralization
c. Job enlargement
d. Delayering

8. _____ is an attempt to motivate employees by giving them the opportunity to use the range of their abilities. It is an idea that was developed by the American psychologist Frederick Herzberg in the 1950s. It can be contrasted to job enlargement which simply increases the number of tasks without changing the challenge.
a. Catfish effect
b. C-A-K-E
c. Cash cow
d. Job enrichment

9. _____ is an approach to management development where an individual is moved through a schedule of assignments designed to give him or her a breadth of exposure to the entire operation.

_____ is also practiced to allow qualified employees to gain more insights into the processes of a company, and to reduce boredom and increase job satisfaction through job variation.

The term _____ can also mean the scheduled exchange of persons in offices, especially in public offices, prior to the end of incumbency or the legislative period.

a. 28-hour day
b. 1990 Clean Air Act
c. 33 Strategies of War
d. Job rotation

10. In operant conditioning, _____ occurs when an event following a response causes an increase in the probability of that response occurring in the future. Response strength can be assessed by measures such as the frequency with which the response is made (for example, a pigeon may peck a key more times in the session), or the speed with which it is made (for example, a rat may run a maze faster.) The environment change contingent upon the response is called a reinforcer.
a. Diminishing Manufacturing Sources and Material Shortages
b. Historiometry
c. Reinforcement
d. Meetings, Incentives, Conferences, and Exhibitions

11. _____ describes how content an individual is with his or her job.

Chapter 13. Motivating Employees

The happier people are within their job, the more satisfied they are said to be. _____ is not the same as motivation, although it is clearly linked.

a. Human relations
b. Job analysis
c. Goal-setting theory
d. Job satisfaction

12. _____ is the state or fact of exclusive rights and control over property, which may be an object, land/real estate or intellectual property. An _____ right is also referred to as title. The concept of _____ has existed for thousands of years and in all cultures.

a. A4e
b. Emanation of the state
c. Ownership
d. A Stake in the Outcome

Chapter 14. Developing Leadership Skills

1. _____ has been described as the 'process of social influence in which one person can enlist the aid and support of others in the accomplishment of a common task' . A definition more inclusive of followers comes from Alan Keith of Genentech who said '_____ is ultimately about creating a way for people to contribute to making something extraordinary happen.'

_____ is one of the most salient aspects of the organizational context. However, defining _____ has been challenging.

   a. Situational leadership
   b. 1990 Clean Air Act
   c. 28-hour day
   d. Leadership

2. _____ and Theory Y are theories of human motivation created and developed by Douglas McGregor at the MIT Sloan School of Management in the 1960s that have been used in human resource management, organizational behavior, organizational communication and organizational development. They describe two very different attitudes toward workforce motivation. McGregor felt that companies followed either one or the other approach.

In _____, which many managers practice, management assumes employees are inherently lazy and will avoid work if they can. They inherently dislike work. Because of this, workers need to be closely supervised and comprehensive systems of controls developed.

   a. Job enrichment
   b. Theory X
   c. Management team
   d. Cash cow

3. Theory X and _____ are theories of human motivation created and developed by Douglas McGregor at the MIT Sloan School of Management in the 1960s that have been used in human resource management, organizational behavior, organizational communication and organizational development. They describe two very different attitudes toward workforce motivation. McGregor felt that companies followed either one or the other approach.

In _____, management assumes employees may be ambitious and self-motivated and exercise self-control. It is believed that employees enjoy their mental and physical work duties.

   a. Design leadership
   b. Theory Y
   c. Business Workflow Analysis
   d. Contingency theory

Chapter 14. Developing Leadership Skills

4. A _____ is a prediction that directly or indirectly causes itself to become true, by the very terms of the prophecy itself, due to positive feedback between belief and behavior. Although examples of such prophecies can be found in literature as far back as ancient Greece and ancient India, it is 20th-century sociologist Robert K. Merton who is credited with coining the expression '_____' and formalizing its structure and consequences. In his book Social Theory and Social Structure, Merton gives as a feature of the _____:

In other words, a prophecy declared as truth when it is actually false may sufficiently influence people, either through fear or logical confusion, so that their reactions ultimately fulfill the once-false prophecy.

   a. 33 Strategies of War
   b. 28-hour day
   c. 1990 Clean Air Act
   d. Self-fulfilling prophecy

5. In psychology, _____ is a major approach to the study of human personality. Trait theorists are primarily interested in the measurement of traits, which can be defined as habitual patterns of behavior, thought, and emotion. According to this perspective, traits are relatively stable over time, differ among individuals (e.g. some people are outgoing whereas others are shy), and influence behavior.
   a. Trait theory
   b. Cognitive dissonance
   c. Psychological statistics
   d. Psychometrics

6. _____ is a term used to describe a policy of allowing events to take their own course. The term is a French phrase literally meaning 'let do'. It is a doctrine that states that government generally should not intervene in the marketplace.
   a. Deep ecology
   b. Freedom of contract
   c. Laissez-faire
   d. Libertarian

7. A _____ is a research instrument consisting of a series of questions and other prompts for the purpose of gathering information from respondents. Although they are often designed for statistical analysis of the responses, this is not always the case. The _____ was invented by Sir Francis Galton.
   a. Questionnaire construction
   b. Mystery shoppers
   c. Structured interview
   d. Questionnaire

Chapter 14. Developing Leadership Skills

8. _____ refers to techniques, processes and tools for organizing and coordinating a group of individuals working towards a common goal--i.e. a team.

Several well-known approaches to _____ have come out of academic work. Examples include the Belbin Team Inventory by Meredith Belbin, a method to identify the different types of personalities within teams, and Ken Blanchard's description of 'High Performing Teams'.

   a. 1990 Clean Air Act
   b. 33 Strategies of War
   c. 28-hour day
   d. Team management

9. Various _____ can be employed dependent on the culture of the business, the nature of the task, the nature of the workforce and the personality and skills of the leaders. This idea was further developed by Robert Tannenbaum and Warren H. Schmidt (1958, 1973) who argued that the style of leadership is dependent upon the prevailing circumstance; therefore leaders should exercise a range of leadership styles and should deploy them as appropriate.

An Autocratic or authoritarian manager makes all the decisions, keeping the information and decision making among the senior management.

   a. 1990 Clean Air Act
   b. Management styles
   c. 33 Strategies of War
   d. 28-hour day

10. The _____ is a leadership theory in the field of organizational studies developed by Robert House in 1971 and revised in 1996. The theory that a leader's behavior is contingent to the satisfaction, motivation and performance of subordinates. The revised version also argues that the leader engage in behaviors that complement subordinate's abilities and compensate for deficiencies.
   a. Human relations
   b. Corporate Culture
   c. Path-goal theory
   d. Sociotechnical systems

11. Contingency leadership theory in organizational studies is a type of leadership theory, leadership style, and leadership model that presumes that different leadership styles are contingent to different situations. It is also referred as _____ Â® theory although, as originally convened, the situational theory term is much more restrictive. The original situational theory argues that the best type of leadership is totally determined by the situational variables.Currently there are many styles of leadership.

a. Situational theory
b. 1990 Clean Air Act
c. Situational leadership
d. 28-hour day

12. _____ is an approach to leadership development, coined and defined by Robert Greenleaf and advanced by several authors such as Stephen Covey, Peter Block, Peter Senge, Max DePree, Margaret Wheatley, Ken Blanchard, and others. Servant-leadership emphasizes the leader's role as steward of the resources (human, financial and otherwise) provided by the organization. It encourages leaders to serve others while staying focused on achieving results in line with the organization's values and integrity.
    a. Adam Smith
    b. Abraham Harold Maslow
    c. Affiliation
    d. Servant leadership

13. _____ is a term used to classify a group leadership theories that inquire the interactions between leaders and followers. A transactional leader focuses more on a series of 'transactions'. This person is interested in looking out for oneself, having exchange benefits with their subordinates and clarify a sense of duty with rewards and punishments to reach goals.
    a. 33 Strategies of War
    b. Transactional leadership
    c. 1990 Clean Air Act
    d. 28-hour day

14. _____ is a leadership style that defines as leadership that creates voluble and positive change in the followers. A transformational leader focuses on 'transforming' others to help each other, to look out for each other, be encouraging, harmonious, and look out for the organization as a whole. In this leadership, the leader enhances the motivation, moral and performance of his follower group.
    a. Transformational leadership
    b. Polynomial conjoint measurement
    c. SESAMO
    d. Strong-Campbell Interest Inventory

Chapter 15. Managing Conflict and Stress

1. A _____ or labor union is an organization of workers who have banded together to achieve common goals in key areas and working conditions. The _____, through its leadership, bargains with the employer on behalf of union members (rank and file members) and negotiates labor contracts (Collective bargaining) with employers. This may include the negotiation of wages, work rules, complaint procedures, rules governing hiring, firing and promotion of workers, benefits, workplace safety and policies.

   a. Working time
   b. Company union
   c. Labour law
   d. Trade union

2. _____ is the harmful physical and emotional response that occurs when there is a poor match between job demands and the capabilities, resources, or needs of the worker.

   Stress-related disorders encompass a broad array of conditions, including psychological disorders (e.g., depression, anxiety, post-traumatic stress disorder) and other types of emotional strain (e.g., dissatisfaction, fatigue, tension, etc.), maladaptive behaviors (e.g., aggression, substance abuse), and cognitive impairment (e.g., concentration and memory problems.) In turn, these conditions may lead to poor work performance or even injury.

   a. 1990 Clean Air Act
   b. Workplace stress
   c. 33 Strategies of War
   d. 28-hour day

3. _____ is a state of discord caused by the actual or perceived opposition of needs, values and interests between people working together. Conflict takes many forms in organizations. There is the inevitable clash between formal authority and power and those individuals and groups affected.

   a. A Stake in the Outcome
   b. A4e
   c. AAAI
   d. Organizational conflict

4. _____ is a range of processes aimed at alleviating or eliminating sources of conflict. The term '_____' is sometimes used interchangeably with the term dispute resolution or alternative dispute resolution. Processes of _____ generally include negotiation, mediation and diplomacy.

   a. 28-hour day
   b. 1990 Clean Air Act
   c. 33 Strategies of War
   d. Conflict resolution

Chapter 15. Managing Conflict and Stress

5. The 'business case for _____', theorizes that in a global marketplace, a company that employs a diverse workforce (both men and women, people of many generations, people from ethnically and racially diverse backgrounds etc.) is better able to understand the demographics of the marketplace it serves and is thus better equipped to thrive in that marketplace than a company that has a more limited range of employee demographics.

An additional corollary suggests that a company that supports the _____ of its workforce can also improve employee satisfaction, productivity and retention.

   a. Trademark
   b. Virtual team
   c. Diversity
   d. Kanban

6. The general definition of an _____ is an evaluation of a person, organization, system, process, project or product. _____s are performed to ascertain the validity and reliability of information; also to provide an assessment of a system's internal control. The goal of an _____ is to express an opinion on the person / organization/system (etc) in question, under evaluation based on work done on a test basis.
   a. A Stake in the Outcome
   b. Audit committee
   c. Internal control
   d. Audit

7. _____ are employee benefit programs offered by many employers, typically in conjunction with a health insurance plan. _____s are intended to help employees deal with personal problems that might adversely impact their work performance, health, and well-being. _____s generally include assessment, short-term counseling and referral services for employees and their household members.
   a. A Stake in the Outcome
   b. A4e
   c. Employee benefits
   d. Employee Assistance Programs

8. Organizational culture is not the same as _____. It is wider and deeper concepts, something that an organization 'is' rather than what it 'has' (according to Buchanan and Huczynski.)

_____ is the total sum of the values, customs, traditions and meanings that make a company unique.

a. Corporate culture
b. Job analysis
c. Work design
d. Path-goal theory

9. In the field of human resource management, _____ is the field concerned with organizational activity aimed at bettering the performance of individuals and groups in organizational settings. It has been known by several names, including employee development, human resource development, and learning and development.

Harrison observes that the name was endlessly debated by the Chartered Institute of Personnel and Development during its review of professional standards in 1999/2000.

a. Person specification
b. Performance appraisal
c. Revolving door syndrome
d. Training and development

10. _____ is the negative psychological link between people and the introduction of new technologies. Whereas ergonomics is the study of how humans react and physically fit with machines in their environment, _____ is, in many ways, the resistance of change that accompanies newly introduced machines to work, home, and leisure situations.

Craig Brod, a leader in the field of _____ research, states that _____ is '...a modern disease of adaptation caused by an inability to cope with the new computer technologies in a healthy manner.'[1] _____ is based on the irrational fear of change.

a. 33 Strategies of War
b. 28-hour day
c. 1990 Clean Air Act
d. Technostress

Chapter 16. Managing Change and Culture

1. Organizational culture is not the same as _____. It is wider and deeper concepts, something that an organization 'is' rather than what it 'has' (according to Buchanan and Huczynski.)

_____ is the total sum of the values, customs, traditions and meanings that make a company unique.

   a. Corporate culture
   b. Job analysis
   c. Work design
   d. Path-goal theory

2. _____ is an influential development in the field of social science. It provides a framework for looking at the factors (forces) that influence a situation, originally social situations. It looks at forces that are either driving movement toward a goal (helping forces) or blocking movement toward a goal (hindering forces.)

   a. Dynamic Enterprise Modeling
   b. Board of governors
   c. Logistics management
   d. Force field analysis

3. _____ is a structured approach to transitioning individuals, teams, and organizations from a current state to a desired future state. The current definition of _____ includes both organizational _____ processes and individual _____ models, which together are used to manage the people side of change.

A number of models are available for understanding the transitioning of individuals through the phases of _____ and strengthening organizational development initiative in both government and corporate sectors.

   a. 28-hour day
   b. 33 Strategies of War
   c. 1990 Clean Air Act
   d. Change management

4. _____ is the harmful physical and emotional response that occurs when there is a poor match between job demands and the capabilities, resources, or needs of the worker.

Stress-related disorders encompass a broad array of conditions, including psychological disorders (e.g., depression, anxiety, post-traumatic stress disorder) and other types of emotional strain (e.g., dissatisfaction, fatigue, tension, etc.), maladaptive behaviors (e.g., aggression, substance abuse), and cognitive impairment (e.g., concentration and memory problems.) In turn, these conditions may lead to poor work performance or even injury.

Chapter 16. Managing Change and Culture

a. 33 Strategies of War
b. 1990 Clean Air Act
c. 28-hour day
d. Workplace stress

5. In the field of human resource management, _____ is the field concerned with organizational activity aimed at bettering the performance of individuals and groups in organizational settings. It has been known by several names, including employee development, human resource development, and learning and development.

Harrison observes that the name was endlessly debated by the Chartered Institute of Personnel and Development during its review of professional standards in 1999/2000.

a. Performance appraisal
b. Person specification
c. Revolving door syndrome
d. Training and development

6. _____ has been described as the 'process of social influence in which one person can enlist the aid and support of others in the accomplishment of a common task'. A definition more inclusive of followers comes from Alan Keith of Genentech who said '_____ is ultimately about creating a way for people to contribute to making something extraordinary happen.'

_____ is one of the most salient aspects of the organizational context. However, defining _____ has been challenging.

a. 1990 Clean Air Act
b. 28-hour day
c. Situational leadership
d. Leadership

7. As defined by Richard Beckhard, _____ is a planned, top-down, organization-wide effort to increase the organization's effectiveness and health. _____ is achieved through interventions in the organization's 'processes,' using behavioural science knowledge. According to Warren Bennis, _____ is a complex strategy intended to change the beliefs, attitudes, values, and structure of organizations so that they can better adapt to new technologies, markets, and challenges.

a. Organizational development
b. Organizational structure
c. Informal organization
d. Organizational culture

8. _____ describes the situation when output from (or information about the result of) an event or phenomenon in the past will influence the same event/phenomenon in the present or future. When an event is part of a chain of cause-and-effect that forms a circuit or loop, then the event is said to 'feed back' into itself.

_____ is also a synonym for:

- _____ signal; the information about the initial event that is the basis for subsequent modification of the event.
- _____ loop; the causal path that leads from the initial generation of the _____ signal to the subsequent modification of the event.

_____ is a mechanism, process or signal that is looped back to control a system within itself. Such a loop is called a _____ loop.

a. Feedback
b. Feedback loop
c. 1990 Clean Air Act
d. Positive feedback

9. _____ is a form of training that claims to make people more aware of their own prejudices, and more sensitive to others. According to its critics, it involves the use of psychological techniques with groups that its critics claim are often identical to brainwashing tactics. Critics believe these techniques are unethical.
a. 33 Strategies of War
b. 1990 Clean Air Act
c. 28-hour day
d. Sensitivity training

10. A _____ is the term given to a company that facilitates the learning of its members and continuously transforms itself. _____s develop as a result of the pressures facing modern organizations and enables them to remain competitive in the business environment. A _____ has five main features; systems thinking, personal mastery, mental models, shared vision and team learning.

a. Quality function deployment
b. Hoshin Kanri
c. 1990 Clean Air Act
d. Learning organization

11. _____ is best described as the process from which managers learn and improve their skills not only to benefit themselves but also their employing organizations.

In organisational development (OD), the effectiveness of management is recognised as one of the determinants of organisational success. Therefore, investment in _____ can have a direct economic benefit to the organization.

a. Job enrichment
b. Management development
c. Senior management
d. Fix it twice

12. In sociology, anthropology and cultural studies, a _____ is a group of people with a culture (whether distinct or hidden) which differentiates them from the larger culture to which they belong. If a particular _____ is characterized by a systematic opposition to the dominant culture, it may be described as a counterculture.

As early as 1950, David Riesman distinguished between a majority, 'which passively accepted commercially provided styles and meanings, and a '_____' which actively sought a minority style ...

a. 33 Strategies of War
b. Subculture
c. 28-hour day
d. 1990 Clean Air Act

Chapter 17. Management Control

1. _____ is one of the managerial functions like planning, organizing, staffing and directing. It is an important function because it helps to check the errors and to take the corrective action so that deviation from standards are minimized and stated goals of the organization are achieved in desired manner. According to modern concepts, _____ is a foreseeing action whereas earlier concept of _____ was used only when errors were detected. _____ in management means setting standards, measuring actual performance and taking corrective action.

   a. Control
   b. Schedule of reinforcement
   c. Turnover
   d. Decision tree pruning

2. _____ describes the situation when output from (or information about the result of) an event or phenomenon in the past will influence the same event/phenomenon in the present or future. When an event is part of a chain of cause-and-effect that forms a circuit or loop, then the event is said to 'feed back' into itself.

   _____ is also a synonym for:

   - _____ signal; the information about the initial event that is the basis for subsequent modification of the event.
   - _____ loop; the causal path that leads from the initial generation of the _____ signal to the subsequent modification of the event.

   _____ is a mechanism, process or signal that is looped back to control a system within itself. Such a loop is called a _____ loop.

   a. 1990 Clean Air Act
   b. Feedback
   c. Feedback loop
   d. Positive feedback

3. Engineering _____ is the permissible limit of variation in

   1. a physical dimension,
   2. a measured value or physical property of a material, manufactured object, system, or service,
   3. other measured values (such as temperature, humidity, etc.)
   4. in engineering and safety, a physical distance or space (_____), as in a truck (lorry), train or boat under a bridge as well as a train in a tunnel

Dimensions, properties, or conditions may vary within certain practical limits without significantly affecting functioning of equipment or a process. _____s are specified to allow reasonable leeway for imperfections and inherent variability without compromising performance.

Chapter 17. Management Control

The _____ may be specified as a factor or percentage of the nominal value, a maximum deviation from a nominal value, an explicit range of allowed values, be specified by a note or published standard with this information, or be implied by the numeric accuracy of the nominal value. _____ can be symmetrical, as in 40±0.1, or asymmetrical, such as 40+0.2/−0.1.

a. Zero defects
b. Quality assurance
c. Root cause analysis
d. Tolerance

4. In economics, business, retail, and accounting, a _____ is the value of money that has been used up to produce something, and hence is not available for use anymore. In economics, a _____ is an alternative that is given up as a result of a decision. In business, the _____ may be one of acquisition, in which case the amount of money expended to acquire it is counted as _____.

a. Cost allocation
b. Fixed costs
c. Cost overrun
d. Cost

5. _____ is an area of business concerned with the production of goods and services, and involves the responsibility of ensuring that business operations are efficient in terms of using as little resource as needed, and effective in terms of meeting customer requirements. It is concerned with managing the process that converts inputs (in the forms of materials, labour and energy) into outputs (in the form of goods and services.)

Operations traditionally refers to the production of goods and services separately, although the distinction between these two main types of operations is increasingly difficult to make as manufacturers tend to merge product and service offerings.

a. A Stake in the Outcome
b. Operations management
c. AAAI
d. A4e

6. _____ generally refers to a list of all planned expenses and revenues. It is a plan for saving and spending. A _____ is an important concept in microeconomics, which uses a _____ line to illustrate the trade-offs between two or more goods.

a. 33 Strategies of War
b. 1990 Clean Air Act
c. 28-hour day
d. Budget

7. _____ is a financial ratio that indicates the percentage of a company's assets are provided via debt. It is the ratio of total debt (the sum of current liabilities and long-term liabilities) and total assets (the sum of current assets, fixed assets, and other assets such as 'goodwill'.)

$$\text{Debt ratio} = \frac{\text{Total Debt}}{\text{Total Assets}}$$

or alternatively:

$$\text{Debt ratio} = \frac{\text{Total Liability}}{\text{Total Assets}}$$

For example, a company with $2 million in total assets and $500,000 in total liabilities would have a _____ of 25%

Like all financial ratios, a company's _____ should be compared with their industry average or other competing firms.

a. Demand forecasting
b. Debt ratio
c. 1990 Clean Air Act
d. 28-hour day

8. In finance, a _____ or accounting ratio is a ratio of two selected numerical values taken from an enterprise's financial statements. There are many standard ratios used to try to evaluate the overall financial condition of a corporation or other organization. _____s may be used by managers within a firm, by current and potential shareholders (owners) of a firm, and by a firm's creditors.
a. Return on sales
b. Rate of return
c. Return on equity
d. Financial ratio

Chapter 17. Management Control

9. In finance, _____ is borrowing money to supplement existing funds for investment in such a way that the potential positive or negative outcome is magnified and/or enhanced. It generally refers to using borrowed funds, or debt, so as to attempt to increase the returns to equity. Deleveraging is the action of reducing borrowings.

   a. Private equity
   b. Limited liability corporation
   c. Limited partners
   d. Gearing

10. Market _____ is a business, economics or investment term that refers to an asset's ability to be easily converted through an act of buying or selling without causing a significant movement in the price and with minimum loss of value. Money, or cash on hand, is the most liquid asset. An act of exchange of a less liquid asset with a more liquid asset is called liquidation.

    a. 1990 Clean Air Act
    b. 28-hour day
    c. 33 Strategies of War
    d. Liquidity

11. An _____ is any party that makes an investment.

The term has taken on a specific meaning in finance to describe the particular types of people and companies that regularly purchase equity or debt securities for financial gain in exchange for funding an expanding company. Less frequently, the term is applied to parties who purchase real estate, currency, commodity derivatives, personal property, or other assets.

   a. AAAI
   b. Investor
   c. A4e
   d. A Stake in the Outcome

12. The _____ is a performance management tool for measuring whether the smaller-scale operational activities of a company are aligned with its larger-scale objectives in terms of vision and strategy.

By focusing not only on financial outcomes but also on the operational, marketing and developmental inputs to these, the _____ helps provide a more comprehensive view of a business, which in turn helps organizations act in their best long-term interests. This tool is also being used to address business response to climate change and greenhouse gas emissions.

a. Management development
b. Commercial management
c. Middle management
d. Balanced scorecard

13. _____ is a process of agreeing upon objectives within an organization so that management and employees agree to the objectives and understand what they are in the organization.

The term '_____' was first popularized by Peter Drucker in his 1954 book 'The Practice of Management'.

The essence of _____ is participative goal setting, choosing course of actions and decision making.

a. Job enrichment
b. Management by objectives
c. Business economics
d. Clean sheet review

14. The general definition of an _____ is an evaluation of a person, organization, system, process, project or product. _____s are performed to ascertain the validity and reliability of information; also to provide an assessment of a system's internal control. The goal of an _____ is to express an opinion on the person / organization/system (etc) in question, under evaluation based on work done on a test basis.
a. Audit
b. A Stake in the Outcome
c. Internal control
d. Audit committee

15. A _____ is a subset of the overall internal controls of a business covering the application of people, documents, technologies, and procedures by management accountants to solving business problems such as costing a product, service or a business-wide strategy. _____s are distinct from regular information systems in that they are used to analyze other information systems applied in operational activities in the organization. Academically, the term is commonly used to refer to the group of information management methods tied to the automation or support of human decision making, e.g. Decision Support Systems, Expert systems, and Executive information systems.
a. Strategic information system
b. Management information system
c. 1990 Clean Air Act
d. 28-hour day

Chapter 18. Appraising and Rewarding Performance

1. _____ is a method by which the job performance of an employee is evaluated _____ is a part of career development.

_____s are regular reviews of employee performance within organizations

Generally, the aims of a _____ are to:

- Give feedback on performance to employees.
- Identify employee training needs.
- Document criteria used to allocate organizational rewards.
- Form a basis for personnel decisions: salary increases, promotions, disciplinary actions, etc.
- Provide the opportunity for organizational diagnosis and development.
- Facilitate communication between employee and administraton
- Validate selection techniques and human resource policies to meet federal Equal Employment Opportunity requirements.

A common approach to assessing performance is to use a numerical or scalar rating system whereby managers are asked to score an individual against a number of objectives/attributes. In some companies, employees receive assessments from their manager, peers, subordinates and customers while also performing a self assessment.

   a. Progressive discipline
   b. Human resource management
   c. Performance appraisal
   d. Personnel management

2. _____ is one of the managerial functions like planning, organizing, staffing and directing. It is an important function because it helps to check the errors and to take the corrective action so that deviation from standards are minimized and stated goals of the organization are achieved in desired manner. According to modern concepts, _____ is a foreseeing action whereas earlier concept of _____ was used only when errors were detected. _____ in management means setting standards, measuring actual performance and taking corrective action.

   a. Decision tree pruning
   b. Schedule of reinforcement
   c. Turnover
   d. Control

3. In human resources or industrial/organizational psychology, _____' 'multisource feedback,' or 'multisource assessment,' is feedback that comes from all around an employee. '360' refers to the 360 degrees in a circle, with an individual figuratively in the center of the circle. Feedback is provided by subordinates, peers, and supervisors.

Chapter 18. Appraising and Rewarding Performance

a. Job knowledge
b. Personnel management
c. Revolving door syndrome
d. 360-degree feedback

4. _____ describes the situation when output from (or information about the result of) an event or phenomenon in the past will influence the same event/phenomenon in the present or future. When an event is part of a chain of cause-and-effect that forms a circuit or loop, then the event is said to 'feed back' into itself.

_____ is also a synonym for:

- _____ signal; the information about the initial event that is the basis for subsequent modification of the event.
- _____ loop; the causal path that leads from the initial generation of the _____ signal to the subsequent modification of the event.

_____ is a mechanism, process or signal that is looped back to control a system within itself. Such a loop is called a _____ loop.

a. Feedback loop
b. Feedback
c. Positive feedback
d. 1990 Clean Air Act

5. _____ involves establishing specific, measurable and time-targeted objectives. Work on the theory of goal-setting suggests that it's an effective tool for making progress by ensuring that participants in a group with a common goal are clearly aware of what is expected from them if an objective is to be achieved. On a personal level, setting goals is a process that allows people to specify then work towards their own objectives - most commonly with financial or career-based goals.

a. Digital strategy
b. Resource-based view
c. Catfish effect
d. Goal setting

6. _____ is a process of agreeing upon objectives within an organization so that management and employees agree to the objectives and understand what they are in the organization.

The term '_____' was first popularized by Peter Drucker in his 1954 book 'The Practice of Management'.

The essence of _____ is participative goal setting, choosing course of actions and decision making.

Chapter 18. Appraising and Rewarding Performance

   a. Business economics
   b. Clean sheet review
   c. Management by objectives
   d. Job enrichment

7. In psychology research on behaviorism, _____ are scales used to report performance. _____ are normally presented vertically with scale points ranging from five to nine.

It is an appraisal method that aims to combine the benefits of narratives, critical incident incidents, and quantified ratings by anchoring a quantified scale with specific narrative examples of good or poor performance.

   a. 1990 Clean Air Act
   b. 28-hour day
   c. 33 Strategies of War
   d. Behaviorally anchored rating scales

8. A _____ is a set of categories designed to elicit information about a quantitative or a qualitative attribute. In the social sciences, common examples are the Likert scale and 1-10 _____s in which a person selects the number which is considered to reflect the perceived quality of a product.

A _____ is an instrument that requires the rater to assign the rated object that have numerals assigned to them.

   a. Spearman-Brown prediction formula
   b. Polytomous Rasch model
   c. Thurstone scale
   d. Rating scale

9. _____ is one of the four elements of marketing mix. An organization or set of organizations (go-betweens) involved in the process of making a product or service available for use or consumption by a consumer or business user.

The other three parts of the marketing mix are product, pricing, and promotion.

   a. Missing completely at random
   b. Matching theory
   c. Job creation programs
   d. Distribution

Chapter 18. Appraising and Rewarding Performance

10. A _____ is a list of the general tasks and responsibilities of a position. Typically, it also includes to whom the position reports, specifications such as the qualifications needed by the person in the job, salary range for the position, etc. A _____ is usually developed by conducting a job analysis, which includes examining the tasks and sequences of tasks necessary to perform the job.
    a. Recruitment Process Insourcing
    b. Job description
    c. Recruitment advertising
    d. Recruitment

11. The _____ refers to a cognitive bias whereby the perception of a particular trait is influenced by the perception of the former traits in a sequence of interpretations.

    Edward L. Thorndike was the first to support the _____ with empirical research. In a psychology study published in 1920, Thorndike asked commanding officers to rate their soldiers; Thorndike found high cross-correlation between all positive and all negative traits.

    a. Sunk costs
    b. Halo effect
    c. Distinction bias
    d. Cognitive biases

12. The _____ was a landmark piece of legislation in the United States that outlawed racial segregation in schools, public places, and employment.
    a. Negligence in employment
    b. Design patent
    c. Financial Security Law of France
    d. Civil Rights Act of 1964

13. _____ is a term describing performance-related pay, most frequently in the context of educational reform. It provides bonuses for workers who perform their jobs better, according to measurable criteria. In the United States, policy makers are divided on whether _____ should be offered to public school teachers, as is commonly the case in the United Kingdom.
    a. Real wage
    b. Performance-related pay
    c. Profit-sharing agreement
    d. Merit pay

Chapter 19. Operations Management and Planning

1. _____ is an area of business concerned with the production of goods and services, and involves the responsibility of ensuring that business operations are efficient in terms of using as little resource as needed, and effective in terms of meeting customer requirements. It is concerned with managing the process that converts inputs (in the forms of materials, labour and energy) into outputs (in the form of goods and services.)

Operations traditionally refers to the production of goods and services separately, although the distinction between these two main types of operations is increasingly difficult to make as manufacturers tend to merge product and service offerings.

   a. A4e
   b. AAAI
   c. A Stake in the Outcome
   d. Operations management

2. _____ is one of the managerial functions like planning, organizing, staffing and directing. It is an important function because it helps to check the errors and to take the corrective action so that deviation from standards are minimized and stated goals of the organization are achieved in desired manner. According to modern concepts, _____ is a foreseeing action whereas earlier concept of _____ was used only when errors were detected. _____ in management means setting standards, measuring actual performance and taking corrective action.

   a. Decision tree pruning
   b. Turnover
   c. Control
   d. Schedule of reinforcement

3. In probability theory, a probability distribution is called _____ if its cumulative distribution function is _____. This is equivalent to saying that for random variables X with the distribution in question, Pr[X = a] = 0 for all real numbers a, i.e.: the probability that X attains the value a is zero, for any number a. If the distribution of X is _____ then X is called a _____ random variable.

   a. Continuous
   b. Decision tree pruning
   c. Connectionist expert systems
   d. Pay Band

4. _____ or lean production, which is often known simply as 'Lean', is a production practice that considers the expenditure of resources for any goal other than the creation of value for the end customer to be wasteful, and thus a target for elimination. Working from the perspective of the customer who consumes a product or service, 'value' is defined as any action or process that a customer would be willing to pay for. Basically, lean is centered around creating more value with less work.

a. Theory of constraints
b. Lean manufacturing
c. Six Sigma
d. Production line

5. A _____ is a computer program typically used to provide some form of artificial intelligence, which consists primarily of a set of rules about behavior. These rules, termed productions, are a basic representation found useful in AI planning, expert systems and action selection. A _____ provides the mechanism necessary to execute productions in order to achieve some goal for the system.
   a. 1990 Clean Air Act
   b. 33 Strategies of War
   c. 28-hour day
   d. Production system

6. _____ can be defined as the idea generation, concept development, testing and manufacturing or implementation of a physical object or service. _____ers conceptualize and evaluate ideas, making them tangible through products in a more systematic approach. The role of a _____er encompasses many characteristics of the marketing manager, product manager, industrial designer and design engineer.
   a. Adam Smith
   b. Affiliation
   c. Product design
   d. Abraham Harold Maslow

7. _____ is an advertisement in which a particular product specifically mentions a competitor by name for the express purpose of showing why the competitor is inferior to the product naming it.

This should not be confused with parody advertisements, where a fictional product is being advertised for the purpose of poking fun at the particular advertisement, nor should it be confused with the use of a coined brand name for the purpose of comparing the product without actually naming an actual competitor. ('Wikipedia tastes better and is less filling than the Encyclopedia Galactica.')

In the 1980s, during what has been referred to as the cola wars, soft-drink manufacturer Pepsi ran a series of advertisements where people, caught on hidden camera, in a blind taste test, chose Pepsi over rival Coca-Cola.

   a. 28-hour day
   b. 1990 Clean Air Act
   c. Comparative advertising
   d. 33 Strategies of War

Chapter 19. Operations Management and Planning

8. In organizational development (OD), _____ is the application of Socio-Technical Systems principles and techniques to the humanization of work.

The aims of _____ to improved job satisfaction, to improved through-put, to improved quality and to reduced employee problems, e.g., grievances, absenteeism.

Under scientific management people would be directed by reason and the problems of industrial unrest would be appropriately (i.e., scientifically) addressed.

   a. Management process
   b. Work design
   c. Graduate recruitment
   d. Path-goal theory

9. _____s is the science of designing the job, equipment, and workplace to fit the worker. Proper _____ design is necessary to prevent repetitive strain injuries, which can develop over time and can lead to long-term disability.

_____s is concerned with the 'fit' between people and their work.

   a. A Stake in the Outcome
   b. AAAI
   c. Ergonomic
   d. A4e

10. _____ describes the situation when output from (or information about the result of) an event or phenomenon in the past will influence the same event/phenomenon in the present or future. When an event is part of a chain of cause-and-effect that forms a circuit or loop, then the event is said to 'feed back' into itself.

_____ is also a synonym for:

- _____ signal; the information about the initial event that is the basis for subsequent modification of the event.
- _____ loop; the causal path that leads from the initial generation of the _____ signal to the subsequent modification of the event.

_____ is a mechanism, process or signal that is looped back to control a system within itself. Such a loop is called a _____ loop.

Chapter 19. Operations Management and Planning

a. Positive feedback
b. Feedback loop
c. 1990 Clean Air Act
d. Feedback

11. _____ is a cross-disciplinary area concerned with protecting the safety, health and welfare of people engaged in work or employment. The goal of all _____ programs is to foster a work free safe environment. As a secondary effect, it may also protect co-workers, family members, employers, customers, suppliers, nearby communities, and other members of the public who are impacted by the workplace environment.
   a. AAAI
   b. Occupational Safety and Health
   c. A4e
   d. A Stake in the Outcome

12. The _____ is the primary federal law which governs occupational health and safety in the private sector and federal government in the United States. It was enacted by Congress in 1970 and was signed by President Richard Nixon on December 29, 1970. Its main goal is to ensure that employers provide employees with an environment free from recognized hazards, such as exposure to toxic chemicals, excessive noise levels, mechanical dangers, heat or cold stress, or unsanitary conditions.
   a. Unemployment and Farm Relief Act
   b. United States Department of Justice
   c. Unemployment Action Center
   d. Occupational Safety and Health Act

13. _____ can be regarded as an outcome of mental processes (cognitive process) leading to the selection of a course of action among several alternatives. Every _____ process produces a final choice. The output can be an action or an opinion of choice.
   a. Decision making
   b. 28-hour day
   c. 1990 Clean Air Act
   d. 33 Strategies of War

14. A _____ is a type of bar chart that illustrates a project schedule. _____s illustrate the start and finish dates of the terminal elements and summary elements of a project. Terminal elements and summary elements comprise the work breakdown structure of the project.

Chapter 19. Operations Management and Planning

   a. 1990 Clean Air Act
   b. 28-hour day
   c. 33 Strategies of War
   d. Gantt chart

15. The _____, is a mathematically based algorithm for scheduling a set of project activities. It is an important tool for effective project management.

It was developed in the 1950s by the Dupont Corporation at about the same time that General Dynamics and the US Navy were developing the Program Evaluation and Review Technique (PERT) Today, it is commonly used with all forms of projects, including construction, software development, research projects, product development, engineering, and plant maintenance, among others.

   a. 33 Strategies of War
   b. 1990 Clean Air Act
   c. Critical path method
   d. 28-hour day

16. The Program (or Project) Evaluation and Review Technique, commonly abbreviated _____, is a model for project management designed to analyze and represent the tasks involved in completing a given project.

_____ is a method to analyze the involved tasks in completing a given project, specially the time needed to complete each task, and identifying the minimum time needed to complete the total project.

_____ was developed primarily to simplify the planning and scheduling of large and complex projects.

   a. 1990 Clean Air Act
   b. 33 Strategies of War
   c. PERT
   d. 28-hour day

Chapter 19. Operations Management and Planning

17. _____ refers to the movement of cash into or out of a business or financial product. It is usually measured during a specified, finite period of time. Measurement of _____ can be used

- to determine a project's rate of return or value. The time of _____s into and out of projects are used as inputs in financial models such as internal rate of return, and net present value.
- to determine problems with a business's liquidity. Being profitable does not necessarily mean being liquid. A company can fail because of a shortage of cash, even while profitable.
- as an alternate measure of a business's profits when it is believed that accrual accounting concepts do not represent economic realities. For example, a company may be notionally profitable but generating little operational cash (as may be the case for a company that barters its products rather than selling for cash.) In such a case, the company may be deriving additional operating cash by issuing shares evaluating default risk, re-investment requirements, etc.

_____ is a generic term used differently depending on the context. It may be defined by users for their own purposes.

a. Cash flow
b. Sweat equity
c. Gross profit
d. Gross profit margin

18. A _____ is a graph (flow chart) depicting the sequence in which a project's terminal elements are to be completed by showing terminal elements and their dependencies.

The work breakdown structure or the product breakdown structure show the 'part-whole' relations. In contrast, the _____ shows the 'before-after' relations.

a. 28-hour day
b. Project network
c. 1990 Clean Air Act
d. 33 Strategies of War

19. _____ is used to assign the available resources in an economic way. It is part of resource management.

In strategic planning, is a plan for using available resources, for example human resources, especially in the near term, to achieve goals for the future.

a. 33 Strategies of War
b. 28-hour day
c. 1990 Clean Air Act
d. Resource allocation

Chapter 19. Operations Management and Planning

20. A _____ is a common type of chart, that represents an algorithm or process, showing the steps as boxes of various kinds, and their order by connecting these with arrows. _____s are used in analyzing, designing, documenting or managing a process or program in various fields.

The first structured method for documenting process flow, the 'flow process chart', was introduced by Frank Gilbreth to members of ASME in 1921 as the presentation 'Process Charts--First Steps in Finding the One Best Way'.

a. Flowchart
b. 28-hour day
c. 33 Strategies of War
d. 1990 Clean Air Act

21. A _____ is a professional in the field of project management. _____s can have the responsibility of the planning, execution, and closing of any project, typically relating to construction industry, architecture, computer networking, telecommunications or software development.

Many other fields in the production, design and service industries also have _____s.

a. Project management
b. Project engineer
c. Project manager
d. Work package

Chapter 20. Operations Control

1. _____ is one of the managerial functions like planning, organizing, staffing and directing. It is an important function because it helps to check the errors and to take the corrective action so that deviation from standards are minimized and stated goals of the organization are achieved in desired manner. According to modern concepts, _____ is a foreseeing action whereas earlier concept of _____ was used only when errors were detected. _____ in management means setting standards, measuring actual performance and taking corrective action.
   a. Control
   b. Turnover
   c. Schedule of reinforcement
   d. Decision tree pruning

2. _____ is an area of business concerned with the production of goods and services, and involves the responsibility of ensuring that business operations are efficient in terms of using as little resource as needed, and effective in terms of meeting customer requirements. It is concerned with managing the process that converts inputs (in the forms of materials, labour and energy) into outputs (in the form of goods and services.)

   Operations traditionally refers to the production of goods and services separately, although the distinction between these two main types of operations is increasingly difficult to make as manufacturers tend to merge product and service offerings.

   a. AAAI
   b. A4e
   c. A Stake in the Outcome
   d. Operations management

3. In economics, business, retail, and accounting, a _____ is the value of money that has been used up to produce something, and hence is not available for use anymore. In economics, a _____ is an alternative that is given up as a result of a decision. In business, the _____ may be one of acquisition, in which case the amount of money expended to acquire it is counted as _____.
   a. Fixed costs
   b. Cost overrun
   c. Cost allocation
   d. Cost

4. The _____ is given by the United States National Institute of Standards and Technology. Through the actions of the National Productivity Advisory Committee chaired by Jack Grayson, it was established by the Malcolm Baldrige National Quality Improvement Act of 1987 - Public Law 100-107 and named for Malcolm Baldrige, who served as United States Secretary of Commerce during the Reagan administration from 1981 until his 1987 death in a rodeo accident. APQC, , organized the first White House Conference on Productivity, spearheading the creation and design of the _____ in 1987, and jointly administering the award for its first three years.

Chapter 20. Operations Control

    a. Scenario planning
    b. Time and attendance
    c. Malcolm Baldrige National Quality Award
    d. Business Network Transformation

5. _____ refers to planned and systematic production processes that provide confidence in a product's suitability for its intended purpose. Refer to the definition by Merriam-Webster for further information . It is a set of activities intended to ensure that products (goods and/or services) satisfy customer requirements in a systematic, reliable fashion.
    a. Quality assurance
    b. 1990 Clean Air Act
    c. 28-hour day
    d. Risk assessment

6. _____ is a business management strategy aimed at embedding awareness of quality in all organizational processes. _____ has been widely used in manufacturing, education, hospitals, call centers, government, and service industries, as well as NASA space and science programs.

As defined by the International Organization for Standardization (ISO):

> '_____ is a management approach for an organization, centered on quality, based on the participation of all its members and aiming at long-term success through customer satisfaction, and benefits to all members of the organization and to society.' ISO 8402:1994

One major aim is to reduce variation from every process so that greater consistency of effort is obtained. (Royse, D., Thyer, B., Padgett D., ' Logan T., 2006)

    a. 1990 Clean Air Act
    b. Quality management
    c. 28-hour day
    d. Total quality management

7. _____ refers to metrics and measures of output from production processes, per unit of input. Labor _____, for example, is typically measured as a ratio of output per labor-hour, an input. _____ may be conceived of as a metrics of the technical or engineering efficiency of production.
    a. Remanufacturing
    b. Productivity
    c. Value engineering
    d. Master production schedule

Chapter 20. Operations Control

8. _____ can be considered to have three main components: quality control, quality assurance and quality improvement. _____ is focused not only on product quality, but also the means to achieve it. _____ therefore uses quality assurance and control of processes as well as products to achieve more consistent quality.
   a. Quality management
   b. 28-hour day
   c. Total quality management
   d. 1990 Clean Air Act

9. _____ is a Japanese philosophy that focuses on continuous improvement throughout all aspects of life. When applied to the workplace, _____ activities continually improve all functions of a business, from manufacturing to management and from the CEO to the assembly line workers. By improving standardized activities and processes, _____ aims to eliminate waste.
   a. Sensitivity analysis
   b. Kaizen
   c. Cross-docking
   d. Psychological pricing

10. _____ or lean production, which is often known simply as 'Lean', is a production practice that considers the expenditure of resources for any goal other than the creation of value for the end customer to be wasteful, and thus a target for elimination. Working from the perspective of the customer who consumes a product or service, 'value' is defined as any action or process that a customer would be willing to pay for. Basically, lean is centered around creating more value with less work.
    a. Lean manufacturing
    b. Production line
    c. Theory of constraints
    d. Six Sigma

11. _____ is a business management strategy, initially implemented by Motorola, that today enjoys widespread application in many sectors of industry.

    _____ seeks to improve the quality of process outputs by identifying and removing the causes of defects (errors) and variation in manufacturing and business processes. It uses a set of quality management methods, including statistical methods, and creates a special infrastructure of people within the organization ('Black Belts' etc.)

a. Six sigma
b. Theory of constraints
c. Takt time
d. Production line

12. A _____ or business method is a collection of related, structured activities or tasks that produce a specific service or product (serve a particular goal) for a particular customer or customers. It often can be visualized with a flowchart as a sequence of activities.

There are three types of _____ es:

1. Management processes, the processes that govern the operation of a system. Typical management processes include 'Corporate Governance' and 'Strategic Management'.
2. Operational processes, processes that constitute the core business and create the primary value stream. Typical operational processes are Purchasing, Manufacturing, Marketing, and Sales.
3. Supporting processes, which support the core processes. Examples include Accounting, Recruitment, Technical support.

A _____ begins with a customer's need and ends with a customer's need fulfillment. Process oriented organizations break down the barriers of structural departments and try to avoid functional silos.

a. Business process
b. 33 Strategies of War
c. 1990 Clean Air Act
d. 28-hour day

13. _____ is a family of standards for quality management systems. _____ is maintained by ISO, the International Organization for Standardization and is administered by accreditation and certification bodies. The rules are updated, the time and changes in the requirements for quality, motivate change.
a. ISO 9000
b. A4e
c. A Stake in the Outcome
d. AAAI

14. In statistics, _____ is:

- the arithmetic _____
- the expected value of a random variable, which is also called the population _____.

It is sometimes stated that the '_____' '_____'s average. This is incorrect if '_____' is taken in the specific sense of 'arithmetic _____' as there are different types of averages: the _____, median, and mode. Other simple statistical analyses use measures of spread, such as range, interquartile range, or standard deviation. For a real-valued random variable X, the _____ is the expectation of X. Note that not every probability distribution has a defined _____; see the Cauchy distribution for an example.

a. Correlation
b. Statistical inference
c. Control chart
d. Mean

15. The _____ in statistical process control is a tool used to determine whether a manufacturing or business process is in a state of statistical control or not.

If the chart indicates that the process is currently under control then it can be used with confidence to predict the future performance of the process. If the chart indicates that the process being monitored is not in control, the pattern it reveals can help determine the source of variation to be eliminated to bring the process back into control.

a. Time series analysis
b. Simple moving average
c. Failure rate
d. Control chart

16. In engineering and manufacturing, _____ and quality engineering are used in developing systems to ensure products or services are designed and produced to meet or exceed customer requirements. Refer to the definition by Merriam-Webster for further information . These systems are often developed in conjunction with other business and engineering disciplines using a cross-functional approach.

a. Process capability
b. Quality control
c. Single Minute Exchange of Die
d. Statistical process control

17. In decision theory and estimation theory, the _____ of an estimator, $\hat{\theta}$, of an unknown parameter of the distribution, θ, is the expected value of the loss function

$$R(\theta, \hat{\theta}) = \mathbb{E}_\theta L(\theta, \hat{\theta}) = \int L(\theta, \hat{\theta})\, dP_\theta.$$

where dP_θ is a probability measure parametrized by θ.

- For a scalar parameter θ and a quadratic loss function,

$$L(\theta, \hat{\theta}) = (\theta - \hat{\theta})^2$$

the _____ function becomes the mean squared error of the estimate,

$$R(\theta, \hat{\theta}) = E_\theta(\theta - \hat{\theta})^2$$

- In density estimation, the unknown parameter is probability density itself. The loss function is typically chosen to be a norm in an appropriate function space. For example, for L^2 norm,

$$L(f, \hat{f}) = \|f - \hat{f}\|_2^2$$

the _____ function becomes the mean integrated squared error

$$R(f, \hat{f}) = E\|f - \hat{f}\|^2$$

a. Risk
b. Linear model
c. Financial modeling
d. Risk aversion

18. In economics, _____ is the desire to own something and the ability to pay for it. The term _____ signifies the ability or the willingness to buy a particular commodity at a given point of time.
a. 33 Strategies of War
b. 28-hour day
c. 1990 Clean Air Act
d. Demand

Chapter 20. Operations Control

19. _____ is an inventory strategy that strives to improve the return on investment of a business by reducing in-process inventory and its associated carrying costs. To meet _____ objectives, the process relies on signals between different points in the process. This means the process is often driven by a series of signals, or Kanban , which tell production when to make the next part. Kanban are usually 'tickets' but can be simple visual signals, such as the presence or absence of a part on a shelf. Implemented correctly, _____ can dramatically improve a manufacturing organization's return on investment, quality, and efficiency.
   a. 1990 Clean Air Act
   b. 33 Strategies of War
   c. 28-hour day
   d. Just-in-time

20. _____ is a concept related to lean and just-in-time (JIT) production. The Japanese word _____ is a common term meaning 'signboard' or 'billboard'. According to Taiichi Ohno, the man credited with developing JIT, _____ is a means through which JIT is achieved.
   a. Trademark
   b. Risk management
   c. Succession planning
   d. Kanban

21. A barcode (also bar code) is an optical machine-readable representation of data. Originally, _____ represented data in the widths (lines) and the spacings of parallel lines, and may be referred to as linear or 1D (1 dimensional) barcodes or symbologies. They also come in patterns of squares, dots, hexagons and other geometric patterns within images termed 2D (2 dimensional) matrix codes or symbologies.
   a. 28-hour day
   b. 1990 Clean Air Act
   c. Bar codes
   d. 33 Strategies of War

22. A _____ is a computer program typically used to provide some form of artificial intelligence, which consists primarily of a set of rules about behavior. These rules, termed productions, are a basic representation found useful in AI planning, expert systems and action selection. A _____ provides the mechanism necessary to execute productions in order to achieve some goal for the system.
   a. 28-hour day
   b. 33 Strategies of War
   c. 1990 Clean Air Act
   d. Production system

23. _____ is a term used by inventory specialists to describe a level of extra stock that is maintained below the cycle stock to buffer against stockouts. _____ exists to counter uncertainties in supply and demand. _____ is defined as extra units of inventory carried as protection against possible stockouts .(shortfall in raw material or packaging.)
   a. Safety stock
   b. Knowledge worker
   c. Product life cycle
   d. Process automation

24. _____ is a software based production planning and inventory control system used to manage manufacturing processes. Although it is not common nowadays, it is possible to conduct _____ by hand as well.

An _____ system is intended to simultaneously meet three objectives:

- Ensure materials and products are available for production and delivery to customers.
- Maintain the lowest possible level of inventory.
- Plan manufacturing activities, delivery schedules and purchasing activities.

Manufacturing organizations, whatever their products, face the same daily practical problem - that customers want products to be available in a shorter time than it takes to make them. This means that some level of planning is required.

   a. 33 Strategies of War
   b. 1990 Clean Air Act
   c. 28-hour day
   d. Material requirements planning

25. _____ is a list of the raw materials, sub-assemblies, intermediate assemblies, sub-components, components, parts and the quantities of each needed to manufacture an end item (final product) .
   a. Scientific management
   b. Methods-time measurement
   c. Bill of materials
   d. Piece rate

26. A _____ is a plan for production, staffing, inventory, etc. It is usually linked to manufacturing where the plan indicates when and how much of each product will be demanded. This plan quantifies significant processes, parts, and other resources in order to optimize production, to identify bottlenecks, and to anticipate needs and completed goods.

a. Piecework
b. Remanufacturing
c. Value engineering
d. Master production schedule

ANSWER KEY

Chapter 1
1. d 2. d 3. d 4. b 5. c 6. c 7. a 8. d 9. b 10. b
11. c 12. d 13. d 14. a 15. d 16. d 17. d

Chapter 2
1. b 2. d 3. d 4. c 5. d 6. b 7. d 8. b 9. a 10. b
11. a 12. d 13. d 14. b 15. a 16. d 17. d 18. d

Chapter 3
1. a 2. d 3. d 4. a

Chapter 4
1. d 2. d 3. d 4. c 5. d 6. a 7. d

Chapter 5
1. c 2. d 3. d 4. a 5. d 6. d 7. b 8. c 9. d 10. d
11. d 12. b 13. b 14. c 15. a 16. a 17. c 18. b 19. b 20. b
21. d 22. c 23. c 24. a 25. a 26. b 27. d 28. c 29. d 30. c
31. b 32. a

Chapter 6
1. c 2. a 3. b 4. a 5. b 6. d 7. d 8. b 9. c 10. d
11. a 12. b 13. b 14. b 15. d

Chapter 7
1. c 2. d 3. b 4. a 5. a 6. d 7. a 8. d 9. c 10. d
11. a 12. c

Chapter 8
1. d 2. d 3. d 4. d 5. d 6. c 7. d 8. b 9. d 10. a
11. c 12. d 13. d

Chapter 9
1. b 2. a 3. d 4. b 5. b 6. d 7. d 8. c 9. b

Chapter 10
1. a 2. d 3. d 4. d 5. b 6. b

Chapter 11
1. c 2. b 3. c 4. c 5. c 6. d 7. d 8. d 9. d 10. d
11. a 12. d 13. d 14. d 15. d 16. d 17. b 18. d 19. d 20. c
21. d 22. d 23. b 24. c 25. c 26. c 27. c 28. d 29. d 30. d
31. d 32. a

Chapter 12
1. a 2. c 3. d 4. d 5. d 6. b 7. b 8. d 9. d

ANSWER KEY

Chapter 13
1. d   2. c   3. d   4. d   5. d   6. d   7. c   8. d   9. d   10. c
11. d   12. c

Chapter 14
1. d   2. b   3. b   4. d   5. a   6. c   7. d   8. d   9. b   10. c
11. c   12. d   13. b   14. a

Chapter 15
1. d   2. b   3. d   4. d   5. c   6. d   7. d   8. a   9. d   10. d

Chapter 16
1. a   2. d   3. d   4. d   5. d   6. d   7. a   8. a   9. d   10. d
11. b   12. b

Chapter 17
1. a   2. b   3. d   4. d   5. b   6. d   7. b   8. d   9. d   10. d
11. b   12. d   13. b   14. a   15. b

Chapter 18
1. c   2. d   3. d   4. b   5. d   6. c   7. d   8. d   9. d   10. b
11. b   12. d   13. d

Chapter 19
1. d   2. c   3. a   4. b   5. d   6. c   7. c   8. b   9. c   10. d
11. b   12. d   13. a   14. d   15. c   16. c   17. a   18. b   19. d   20. a
21. c

Chapter 20
1. a   2. d   3. d   4. c   5. a   6. d   7. b   8. a   9. b   10. a
11. a   12. a   13. a   14. d   15. d   16. b   17. a   18. d   19. d   20. d
21. c   22. d   23. a   24. d   25. c   26. d

www.ingramcontent.com/pod-product-compliance
Lightning Source LLC
Chambersburg PA
CBHW081846230426
43669CB00018B/2836